EMPHYSEMA

and

COMMON SENSE

by

Spencer H. Robley

Parker Publishing Company, Inc., West Nyack, N.Y.

© 1968 BY

Parker Publishing Company, Inc.
West Nyack, N.Y.

Library of Congress
Catalog Card Number: 68-12361

Fourth Printing . . . . . July, 1979

PRINTED IN THE UNITED STATES OF AMERICA

B & P

To Mary Ellen, whose help, encouragement, and patience made this book possible. As my nurse, she has been at my side throughout all my battles with emphysema. As my helpmate, she has served as my secretary, correcting my reports and typing my manuscripts, and has served as my right arm night and day.

In addition to this she has, somehow, found time to make for our children and for me a healthy, happy home.

A FOREWORD BY A
DOCTOR OF MEDICINE

The author has made an important contribution pertaining to emphysema and its care by writing this book. Because he, himself, is a victim of this insidious progressive condition, he has been able to capture a great deal of insight and understanding of emphysema in the pages of this book. As a victim, he is anxious to relate what has helped him in order that other people, suffering from this condition, will be able to gain from his experience. He, therefore, hopes to keep other victims from getting worse than they are at the time of reading this book.

The author has examined emphysema in all possible aspects. He gives you information from his own personal experience as well as his extensive research into his own health problem. Each chapter has individual meaning and impact for you, the reader. Each reader will want to stop and ponder how the facts and knowledge gained from this book can be specifically applied to himself. The facts, as stated, are accurate. He has made his descriptions understandable and well illustrated to permit the reader to understand clearly the problem of emphysema. In addition to reviewing this manuscript, I have also gained a new perspective of the problems associated with emphysema.

Here is a book which is filled with positive suggestions as to how emphysema sufferers can help themselves to live a more satisfying life. It is also a "handbook" for the physician and others, who become involved in caring for those who have this condition. It is reliable and directly simple, making the book useful for technically oriented personnel as well as laymen. It is not intended to be a medical treatise or a compendium of all the technical information available on this subject. It is, however, an excellent information source on emphysema, written by a layman primarily for the consumption and use by you, the emphysema victim.

The book starts out by explaining the anatomy and physiology of the lungs to permit understanding of how you breathe and why you may slowly become worse. The author tells you what he has done to help himself.

One important theme runs through the entire book—you must take care of your entire body and self. Not only need you consider specific treatment for your lungs, but you also must be extremely careful about your diet and living conditions. This "total concept" in caring for emphysema is so vital that I feel impelled to emphasize this as you read the book. Your doctor can combat the infections and acute problems, but he cannot stand by your side and remind you to eat well, exercise, use postural drainage, breathe clean air and take vitamin preparations. These somewhat tedious and time-consuming processes must be done daily and faithfully if you value your health.

With this type of dedication to living your life to the fullest, thousands of you, who are suffering from mild to severe emphysema, can still lead a useful and satisfying life. I approve and highly recommend this book.

Robert A. Elliot, M.D.

ACKNOWLEDGMENTS

The process of accumulating knowledge is such that it is never possible for anyone to say exactly how he acquired it. I now find this circumstance somewhat consoling because, in a very real sense, this book is not my book. It is the product of the many people who over the years have taught me what is written herein.

Obviously, I cannot acknowledge my indebtedness to all these people and sources, so I must limit it to a few who seem to stand out in my past and to those who helped directly with the preparation and checking of the material in this book.

To all the doctors who have treated me throughout my illness I wish to express my thanks, and especially to John Howick, J. A. Coleman, L. S. Greenlea, and Robert A. Elliot.

I appreciate the service of my wife Mary Ellen for typing, Irene Stromberg for assistance in preparation, and Doctor Elliot for his review of the manuscript. A special thanks is for my son, Bryon, who prepared most of the illustrations.

In compiling material for this book, I consulted various standard reference textbooks, such as *Pulmonary Emphysema* by Walter C. Alvarez, M.D., and the *Textbook of Medical Physiology* by Arthur C. Guyton, M.D.

HOW THIS BOOK
CAN HELP YOU

When I first discovered that I had a mysterious malady called emphysema, I was naturally curious to find out something about it. My doctors attempted, in what seemed vague medical terminology, to explain to me how my lungs were becoming distorted and why I was always breathless. I tried reading medical books with little success. Such books include, by necessity, much medical knowledge prerequisite for full understanding. I read many articles on emphysema in current magazines. These articles warned of the rising incidence of emphysema and quoted many statistics. However, when it came to a simple explanation of emphysema and how to treat it, I found no ready answer. As the years passed and I learned little by little about this mystery, I resolved to share my knowledge with other victims of this condition called emphysema.

To really know emphysema, you must experience it as I have. This book tells about emphysema, my experiences with it, its causes, effects, and safe and sane methods of coping with it. The purposes of this book are therefore to report the facts, to make them understandable, and to stimulate their application as stated in the book. Every attempt has been made to be accurate as to reporting the facts. The evaluations, however, belong personally to the author.

The work has been prepared for the general public and especially for the emphysema victim, rather than for the physician. With this purpose in view, medical technicalities have been avoided as far as possible.

Each chapter in the book is adequate and complete in itself. You can profitably read this book, even for 15 to 20 minutes at a time. I have tried to discuss emphysema from every possible aspect, and I have divided the subject matter in such a way that the patient can readily explore material relative to his own problem. The book has illustrations to amplify the text.

If the principles set forth in this book are faithfully followed by emphysema victims, great improvement in health can result. Any training involves much more than merely being "told how." Diligent practice is required for one to put the precepts into effect and to develop the habit of using them.

Your own doctor is the man to see to determine if you have emphysema. I have always felt that emphysema victims should return to their doctors for periodic checkups. Meanwhile, this book maintains that it is possible to do much good for your condition through self-help techniques.

This book has been written for you—my fellow emphysema sufferers—with the sincere hope that you will be helped considerably in coping with your condition by the principles and programs set out in this book.

Spencer H. Robley

CONTENTS

ILLUSTRATIONS

IS THERE
A CURE FOR
EMPHYSEMA?

The puzzling problem of curing emphysema has confronted the medical profession for some time. Since we are to learn that emphysema is in reality a condition and not a disease, it would be better to ask, "Can the condition, health, and overall physical well-being of an emphysema sufferer be improved?" The answer to that question is a definite "YES!"

During my fight with emphysema, doctors have said, "You have the worst pair of lungs I have ever seen." "It's nothing short of a miracle that you are alive." This certainly sounds far from encouraging. But, regardless of the pessimistic attitudes of my doctors, I am still very much alive!

Today, the perfect example of a victim of this malady, I am hollow-cheeked, barrel-chested, hump-backed, thin, and still get that breathless feeling when I walk long distances or climb.

All the terrible ravages of infections which are associated with emphysema have been suffered. I have been racked with coughing until I thought each minute was my last. There were countless sleepless nights when my patient wife

19

sat up with me while I, literally, fought to keep from choking to death.

Throughout all this suffering, I never had any doubt that I could overcome most of the misery connected with emphysema. I am still short of breath after walking a few blocks, but I have been able to *heal* my lungs. The damage to the lung tissues is there, but the continuous infection, the continuous mucus and phlegm, and the incessant fight to barely exist are gone. On some mornings I discharge a small bit of mucus, say, perhaps, a thimble full. But that is all! The constant cough is gone! I lead a reasonably normal life.

It is true that I have a low resistance to infections, and I have to be extremely careful not to expose myself to colds. I have to be vigorous to treat any infections in my lungs with great diligence. However, I know that it is possible for you to overcome 90 per cent of your problems, stop coughing almost entirely, heal those beat-up, old lungs, and improve your ability to breathe so that you can live a reasonably normal life. I did it, and if that is the case, so can you!

As a patient who has 15 years' experience fighting emphysema, I believe I am thoroughly qualified to write with authority about the subject. I am not trying to tell you that I am a doctor, because that is not so. I am trained as an engineer and with this basic technical know-how, I have made my condition an intensive business and personal research program.

I have been treated in various clinics and hospitals, in many doctor's offices, and in my own home. I have spent several of these years in bed when my total attention was turned to a possible cure or some improvement. In view of these facts I believe I know more about emphysema than any doctor, unless that doctor is also a victim of this terrible disorder. This is not said in a boasting way, but I believe that a patient who has suffered for many years from any malady knows more about his particular condition than any doctor can possibly know. This should be particularly true of a patient who has made improvement in the face of great odds. The patient may not know all of the cures, but he certainly knows all the problems. Also, he knows what effect the medicines and treatments have had on him in regard to the problem.

Your interest in this book is a personal one, because you are interested in getting well and improving yourself. This book is written as a "Do" book, not a "Don't" book, and is for those sick people suffering from chronic pulmonary emphysema. I have tried to be positive, telling you what to do to improve, rather than emphasizing the things to avoid. Of course a few don'ts will be included to guide you.

Now the big question, How long will it take to recover? In my case it took many years to heal the lungs. However, if I had been given all the information contained in this book, along with all of the medications now available, I believe I could have made a good recovery in three to four years. This may sound like an impossibly long time, but when you read the material presented in the following chapters and have a better understanding of your lungs and the conditions which bring about emphysema, you will appreciate what an accomplishment it is to improve at all.

I seriously hope that you will benefit in many ways from this publication, because I, the writer and a victim of emphysema, know that any small measure of improvement will be welcomed by thousands suffering from this modern day scourge.

It is my intent to be very frank in the discussion of this problem. I have called a spade, "a spade," so to speak.

Some of the problems involved with a deep lung infection, such as emphysema, do not present a pretty picture. But I believe that if we can get down to the roots of the problem and objectively discuss what happens, the personal feelings involved, and the possible reactions, the patient is going to benefit.

Read this book thoroughly. You will find numerous things which you can try and, thereby, determine whether or not they benefit your condition. I have tried to keep the language simple and understandable, and illustrations are provided to further assist you. Doctors often refer to emphysema patients as "lungers," so I have adopted the reference, lunger, in the writing of this book, not in disrespect, but only to vary the material and make it more readable.

Again I wish to state that I am not a doctor, and I am not trying to take your doctor's place. His orders should always be carried out. Rather, I am simply relating to you, from my own experiences, what has been beneficial. Possibly, this may help you, the reader, suffering from emphysema.

You cannot cure emphysema, but you can learn to live with it. You can master it. You can become and remain a useful, happy, and confident person.

Summary of Chapter I

1. Emphysema is not a disease; it is a condition of the lungs and respiratory system.

2. Although emphysema cannot be cured, the health of the victim can be improved to overcome many of the difficulties associated with this malady.

3. A patient who is the victim of a disease for many years often has a better understanding of his condition than a doctor.

4. It will probably take extensive time to effect noticeable improvement, so do not expect miracles when coping with emphysema.

5. This book is written to assist the emphysema patient to help himself.

6. The author has been a victim of an aggravated case of emphysema for over 15 years.

7. The self-help offered is the result of many years of author's observation, intensive research, and collaboration with doctors.

2

THE FUNCTION
OF THE LUNGS

In the process of living your body uses
oxygen in order to burn the foods you eat and, thereby,
produce energy in your body cells. Blood is used to trans-
port to the body cells both oxygen from the air in the lungs
and food from the stomach. It is pumped by the heart
through passages which end in a maze of extremely small
tubes called capillaries. These feed each body cell.

At the same time the "burning" of food in your body
cells takes place, another gas—carbon dioxide—is produced.
This exhaust from the human machine is transported by
the blood from the body cells to the lungs for expulsion.

In a normal 24-hour day you breathe about 23,040 times,
taking in about 440 cubic feet of air. This supply enables
2,880 gallons of blood, pumped through 100,000 miles of
blood vessels, to furnish oxygen to 300,000 million cells
in your body. That is a lot of work for a pair of lungs which
weigh three to four pounds or about $\frac{1}{40}$ or less of your
total weight.*

Each resting breath you take consists of about a pint of
air, which is approximately $\frac{1}{5}$ oxygen. The other $\frac{4}{5}$ of the
air is a gas called nitrogen. Nitrogen is not used by the

---

* The statistics and information as to size, capacity, etc., in this chapter are
given for normal lungs, not for the diseased or EMPHYSEMATOUS lung.

25

body and simply dilutes the oxygen you breathe for life. This air you breathe travels briefly in your lungs through a maze of branching tubes leading to 600 million tiny air sacs (alveoli). These air sacs are so made that they act as gas exchangers, adding some oxygen to the blood and removing some carbon dioxide gas which is produced by your body as it burns the food you eat to produce energy to walk, run, and carry on all the functions of life.

The expansion of your chest upon breathing in allows air to flow into your lung tubes which end in the air sacs. These tiny air sacs are surrounded by very small blood vessels. The tissues which separate the air sacs and the blood vessels are extremely thin so that oxygen in the air can penetrate them (a process called diffusion) and enter the blood stream. At the same time the waste gas, carbon dioxide, which has been picked up by the blood from the cells, travels out into the sacs and is exhaled as your lungs squeeze out the spent air.

The available surface area of the tissues in the air sacs of your lungs, which is used for the gas exchange process, is huge. If your lungs were spread out they would cover 800 square feet or about two times the floor area of a two car garage. To put it another way, the tissue area of your lungs is 40 times the surface area of your entire body. With this large area oxygen can be added and carbon dioxide can be removed at a very rapid rate.

The function of the lungs not only provides an efficient exchange of oxygen and carbon dioxide, but also removes other products of tissue metabolism, including heat. So your lungs also serve as part of your temperature regulation system similar to air conditioning.

Your breathing apparatus starts with two tubes of the nose and a third, the mouth, which join to become one tube

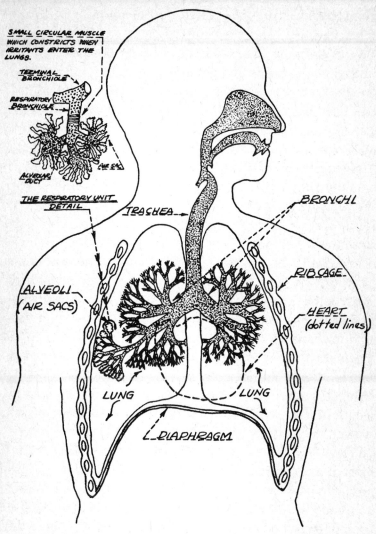

Figure 2-1. A simplified diagram of the lungs and breathing system.

called the trachea. The trachea divides into two tubes, called bronchi; each leading respectively into the right and left lung. Each of these bronchi divides into two, and each of these tubes divides into two more, and so on, so that the number of tubes continue to multiply. One tube divides into 2, 2 tubes divide into 4, 4 into 8, 8 into 16, 16 into 32, etc., until there are 22 subdivisions, resulting in more than a million tubes that each end in many air sacs or alveoli. Each of these air sacs is very small, varying in diameter from 0.003 to 0.013 inches.

When the lungs are emptied by exhaling all of the air possible, they still contain over a quart of air. This is because the tubes in the lung do not collapse. This is referred to medically as the residual volume. When a person breathes, he does not normally force out all the possible air. Thus, at the end of a normal exhalation the lungs contain more than two quarts of air. This is called the functional residual capacity. When the lungs are expanded to the maximum fullness, they contain from six to seven quarts. This is called total capacity.

Regardless of these various measurements of lung capacity, the really important thing is the amount of air that reaches the air sacs (alveoli).

When you are resting you inhale and exhale about ½ quart of air with each breath. When you breathe in, this ½ quart of air is added to the 2 quarts of air which is in your lungs, and supplies just the amount of oxygen which passes through the air sac walls into your blood. At the same time when you breathe out, the ½ quart of spent air contains the volume of carbon dioxide produced by the body cells as it "burns" food to supply energy. So looking at breathing we see that we are really not emptying our lungs completely and filling them with new air, but we are adding to and taking from a reservoir of air which is always in our lungs. Normally an adult breathes from ten to 14 times a

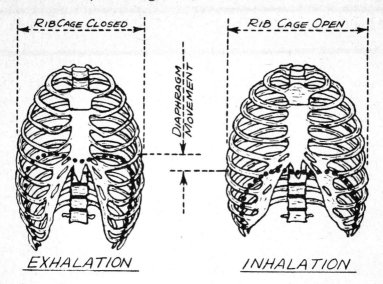

RIB CAGE CLOSED

RIB CAGE OPEN

DIAPHRAGM MOVEMENT

EXHALATION

INHALATION

THE LUNGS ARE LOCATED IN THE THORAX WHICH IS THE
SPACE FORMED BY THE RIB CAGE AND THE DIAPHRAGM, AS
ILLUSTRATED BY THE DOTTED LINE. INHALATION (BREATHING
IN) TAKES PLACE WHEN THE RIB CAGE EXPANDS AND
THE DIAPHRAGM PULLS THE LUNGS OPEN, ALLOWING OUTSIDE
AIR, WHICH IS UNDER PRESSURE, TO RUSH IN. EXHALATION
OCCURS WHEN MUSCLES RELAX AND THE ELASTICITY OF
THE LUNG TISSUES AND RIB MUSCLES SQUEEZES THE
SPENT AIR OUT OF THE LUNGS.

Figure 2-2. The movements of the rib cage.

minute with the resulting volume, called ventilation, of five
to seven quarts per minute. The maximum breathing volume is about 30 times the resting volume, so the normal
lung certainly has a great reserve. It is a remarkable thing
that the proper amount of fresh air reaches up to 600 million air sacs almost simultaneously. The combination of
large area and thin membrane walls of the air sacs is mainly
responsible for much of the lungs' efficiency in the oxygen
and carbon-dioxide gas exchange.

The air all around us is under pressure due to its weight.

At sea level this pressure is about 14 pounds per square inch. When a man breathes, the lungs are expanded and the air pressure in the lungs is reduced so that the air on the outside, which is at a higher pressure, rushes into the lungs through the nose or mouth. The central cavity of the body (the cage-like hole formed by the ribs where the lungs are located) is called the thorax. The lungs are enlarged when you breathe by means of the diaphragm, which is a large dome-shaped muscular tissue covering the lower portion of the thoracic cavity below the lungs. When this dome-shaped muscle contracts, the lungs are pushed downward by air pressure and are thus filled with air. At the same time as you inhale, the rib cage also enlarges somewhat, thus creating a larger space for the lungs to occupy. When you exhale, you simply relax all of the muscles. The elastic tissues return to their normal size, and this squeezes the lungs forcing out the air.

In breathing at rest, the elastic return of the lung tissues accomplishes most of the exhalation. However, when the body is doing work, and especially when heavy work is being performed, muscles in the stomach area and also in the rib cage assist to empty the lungs at exhalation.

Now, if you are in a hospital and need to have more oxygen, you can simply live in a tent in which the atmosphere is pure oxygen, instead of only ⅕ oxygen as in normal air. This will certainly improve the amount of oxygen available to the blood supply. However, supplying oxygen in greater than normal amounts does not increase the volume of gas you inhale and exhale. Therefore, you cannot get rid of more carbon dioxide as the amount of blood being pumped to the cells of your body does not increase.

In the case of lung disease, such as emphysema, the

elimination of carbon dioxide is as important as getting oxygen. Extra oxygen can be of some assistance during short periods of high stress or infection, but it will not in general relieve you much from your everyday breathing problems. Even if you could build a house with an atmosphere of, say, twice as much oxygen as you normally breathe, you probably would not notice much general improvement, because you cannot get rid of twice as much carbon dioxide. Thus extra oxygen is desirable for emergencies, but it is ordinarily of little assistance to the emphysema victim.

A person takes from four to ten million breaths a year and in so doing, draws into the air sacs of his lungs air that is either hot or cold, dry or moist, possibly clean, but probably dirty. Each quart of city air, for instance, contains several million particles of foreign matter. In one day a city dweller may inhale 20 billion such particles. *But, what protects the lungs from this dirt load?* The answer to this important question will be explored in the following paragraphs.

The first duty of the upper tubes of the lungs is to conduct air to and from the lungs proper. These tubes and passages also form a high class air cleaner, conditioner, and filter. The tubes contain a warning device to signal the presence of most air pollutants. Also, they are fitted with a remarkable mechanism which catches and moves the dirt particles upward and out of the lungs at speeds up to one inch per minute.

The upper part of the air passages (nose and sinuses) are lined with a layer of tissue with a rich blood supply to act as a temperature control, either warming or cooling the air as required. The hairs of the nose and the shape of the nasal passages capture the very large dirt particles. The medium sized particles are mostly captured by the walls of the tubes which are completely covered with a sheet of damp slime called *mucus*. Only very fine particles ever reach the air sacs. These fine particles, which are probably not much larger than the air molecules themselves, often stay in suspension in the air and are swept out again by the breathing process.

Foreign bodies which settle in the nose are often expelled by the explosive blast of a sneeze. Particles which settle in the upper tubes of the lungs are often expelled by another kind of blast, which we call a cough. But, more often, they are removed by the cleaning system in the lungs, which is done by the hair-like fingers that line the tubes. These hair-like fingers are called cilia. (One is referred to as a cilium.) They are powered by a mechanism which causes each cilium to make a fast, forceful, forward-stroking movement and a slower, less forceful, backward stroke which returns the cilium to the starting position again. The strokes of the cilia work in a precise manner so that the hairs move together as a wave. The hairs do not work in the air, but are covered with a sheet of damp slime or mucus that is produced by glands among the cilia. The effect of this wave-like motion is to move the entire mucus sheet, containing the trapped dirt particles, up the tubes to the mouth where it can be swallowed or expectorated.

This dirt elevator works all the time, and provides around-the-clock removal of foreign matter from the lungs.

This air conditioning system can remove bacteria and viruses and, unless it is overloaded, the air sacs of the normal healthy lung are kept practically sterile. When irritants penetrate deep into the lungs, the automatic reflex response is usually a cough combined with bronchial air passage constriction. At first, this lung passage shrinking is an effect, which is less obvious than a cough. The normal, healthy person is not aware of this constriction, because it does not affect his conscious nervous system or his ability to breathe.

Air pollutants, smoking, irritating gases, fumes, aerosols, or smog may give rise to air passage constriction. As we have described, each extremely small bronchus (tube) ends in a group of air sacs (alveoli). Each of these small bronchi has a circular muscle located just before the connection to the air sacs. When irritation occurs, this small circular muscle constricts, sometimes partially closing off and often completely closing off the air sacs from the rest of the lung.

Repeated exposure to any of these air pollutants may produce more and more bronchial constriction. This irritation is almost always accompanied by excessive secretion of mucus and, at the same time, a noticeable reduction in the clearing action of the cilia. This combined effect causes the small air passages to become obstructed. In these circumstances bacteria can more readily lodge in the air sacs (alveoli) and remain there long enough to start an infection.

These aforementioned processes are a short but concise description of the start of lung distress, *which may lead to emphysema.* It is a sad fact that the lungs have no restorative powers, that is, new useful lung tissue cannot be grown to take the place of destroyed tissue. For this reason a person with weak or diseased lungs will want to make every effort to prevent further damage caused by irritants and destructive infection. Each attack further reduces the effective area of the lung tissues because more and more alveoli and the associated little tubes leading into the air sacs are destroyed.

Summary of Chapter 2

1. How the normal lungs function; how the breathing process works; how the body cells receive oxygen from the lungs.

2. Normal lung tissues are elastic, similar to a rubber balloon.

3. Breathing out carbon dioxide is a particular problem; stomach muscles can assist in exhaling properly.

4. Healthy lungs have an automatic air-cleaning system. This system removes dirt as well as bacteria and virus.

5. Smoking tobacco, breathing smog and irritants cause early lung disease, loss of elasticity and destruction of the air cleaning system.

6. Extra oxygen may not always be the answer to aggravated breathing problems.

7. The lungs have no restorative powers to replace damaged tissues.

3

EMPHYSEMA— WHAT IS IT?

Emphysema is a new word to most Americans. Twenty years ago it was unheard-of in the layman's vocabulary, and was a term used only by doctors and clinical specialists.

However, today with more attention being given to air pollution in our great cities and the studies on the dangers of smoking, the word "emphysema" is heard and seen quite often. No doubt some people have been suffering from this condition for a long time, and doctors have been calling it by other names. Bronchitis, asthma, and hay fever are a few of the common terms which may have been used. However, one thing seems clear and that is that the lung disorder, which we now know as emphysema, only recently has become widespread enough to be recognized as a special and specific ailment. Also, bearing in mind the stress and pressure of modern living, the habit of smoking tobacco, and air pollution (including smog and man-made dusts), *emphysema is probably the product of modern times.*

Emphysema is not a disease like measles or smallpox, which can be cured. It is a condition, a disorder of the lungs and respiratory system. To understand how to assist yourself and improve your ability to live with emphysema, you must have a good understanding of the disorder and how it affects your daily living processes. In order to reach this understanding I suggest that, in addition to the material in this chapter, you might find it helpful to review Chapter 2.

The lungs work just opposite to the process of blowing up a rubber balloon. When you breathe in (inhale), the muscles about your lungs and diaphragm pull your lungs open, and the air on the outside, which is under pressure, rushes in to fill the void. A condition similar to inhaling would exist if a rubber balloon had hundreds of small strings attached to the rubber skin, and these strings were pulled in the proper direction to open the balloon and allow air to fill it through the neck. Now, when we let go or release all of the strings on our balloon, the rubber will cause the balloon to collapse and squeeze out the air into the atmosphere. This condition is similar to exhaling, because the elastic tissues squeeze the lung closed.

Exhaling requires work because you are pushing out air against the normal air pressure on the outside of your body. When you exhale, the muscles in your chest and diaphragm relax, and the tissues of your lungs, which are elastic like a rubber balloon, collapse and force the old, used air out of your lungs, thus doing work.

Certain muscles in the rib cage and in the stomach area also work to assist in exhalation. Because of breathing difficulties, it is these muscles of exhalation in the stomach area which the emphysema victim must develop and train to assist and offset other lost lung functions.

Now, nobody knows why, but some unlucky persons start to lose this elastic, rubber-like quality in their lungs, and it becomes more and more difficult to squeeze out the old, used air. This is one of the forerunners of emphysema.

Your lungs are continuously cleaned by a flow of fluid called mucus, which keeps the entire inside of them wet.

This liquid gathers up the dirt, dust, virus, bacteria, germs, and other small particles which get into your lungs with the air, and keeps the lungs' tissues clean. The liquid is moved upward by small hair-like fingers called cilia, thousands of which line the passages of your lungs. The cilia move back and forth in unison, similar to a gentle wind moving a field of wheat, and this has the effect of sweeping the liquid up to the throat. Normal people are not conscious of this liquid being discharged, but the motion of clearing the throat before speaking or on other occasions, is actually a conscious help to move the lung liquids up and out.

Emphysema is started by irritation of the lungs. This irritation may be caused by smoking, smog, dirty city air, auto exhausts, pollen, industrial gasses, or infections. When the upper tubes of your lungs are irritated by too much foreign dirt or chemicals, the glands which produce the mucus to wash your lungs start to work faster, thus making a great flood of mucus. This is the very first evidence that something is amiss with the lungs. The first discharge is a semi-liquid, colorless material, which is very corrosive and causes a great deal of coughing, especially in the morning. This material is not very sticky and coughs up quite easily, but there is a great volume of discharge every day. The victim is frequently coughing and spitting mucus. The morning discharge is sometimes so large that it is almost unbelievable.

At the same time this is happening, there is another thing taking place in the lungs which is not so easily detected. When the lung tissues and tubes are irritated, they start to constrict or contract so that the openings become smaller all the way down to the small air sacs. This causes the coughing to become more violent in order to empty the lungs of the flood of mucus.

If the irritation continues, the small "brooms" (cilia), which clean the lungs, become sluggish and their cleaning action becomes less and less efficient. The coughing now must also expel much of the mucus which was formerly swept out by the cilia. The violent coughing fits begin to start lung tissue damage by causing a rupture or tearing of the small air sacs of the lungs. These small air sacs fuse or are joined together to form larger sacs, thus reducing the efficiency of the lungs.

As we have learned, the small tube leading to the air sacs is often closed off by a circular muscle when repeated irritation occurs. When the groups of air sacs are isolated by this muscle constriction, the small air sacs rupture due to violent changes in pressure during coughing. This fusion process continues to some degree as long as irritation exists in the lungs.

Finally, the cleaning of the lungs by the cilia becomes so poor that virus and bacteria (germs) can easily get deep into the lungs and remain to start infections. Also, virus attacks leave the lung tissue with open sores which are easy prey for bacteria. These infections cause the production of pus and other products of infection, similar to what an open wound, cut, or abrasion on your hand would produce. These products must be swept out of the lungs by coughing. However, the material is now more difficult to remove because it is sticky, tends to adhere to the membranes of the lungs, and great effort is required to eject it. The floods of mucus, which the body produced at first in an effort to combat the irritation, slow down. The total effect is to cause the material produced by the lungs to become more and more difficult to eject, thus increasing the coughing effort required.

While all this is going on, the constant coughing and

breathing in a gasping manner is causing the chest cavity and the rib cage to enlarge. It becomes shaped like a barrel, instead of the rather flat shape of the normal chest. As we read in Chapter 2 dealing with the lungs, the main muscle of breathing is the diaphragm, which spreads under the rib cage and is shaped like a dome. When the rib cage of the emphysema victim expands, this sheet of muscle tissue is pulled tighter and is flat or less dome-shaped. The result of the stretching of the diaphragm is that breathing is more difficult because the lungs cannot be emptied or squeezed shut as far as normal lungs can be. (Figure 3-1 illustrates this fact.)

During the process, the muscle tissues in and about the lungs, which squeeze the lung sacs to expel the air, become weakened by constant irritation and coughing. The result is that the rubber-like closing of the lung sacs is reduced immensely.

When lung tissue heals after a sore, due to infection, or tearing of the tissue by coughing, the healed tissue is no longer useful to transfer oxygen to the blood. It is gone forever. As infections in the lungs progress, the tissue becomes filled with tiny areas of scar tissue, which further reduces the lungs' ability to get oxygen from the air into the blood.

The mucus and pus, which is produced by your lungs, is very corrosive, and these products are themselves known to be capable of destroying tissue in the lungs. This corrosive property is partially what may create that burning sensation in your chest when you have a deep cold or infection.

As your lungs enlarge with your chest cavity, they naturally hold more air. And, when you exhale, you have much more air left in your lungs than a normal, healthy person

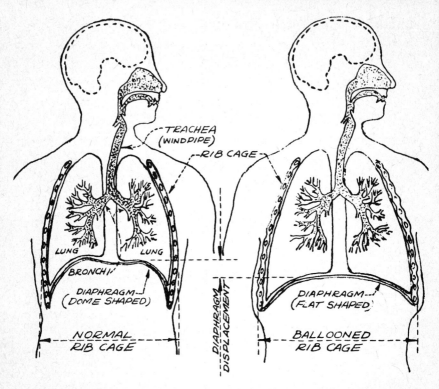

TRACHEA (WINDPIPE)

RIB CAGE

LUNG

LUNG

BRONCHI

DIAPHRAGM (DOME SHAPED)

NORMAL RIB CAGE

DIAPHRAGM DISPLACEMENT

DIAPHRAGM (FLAT SHAPED)

BALLOONED RIB CAGE

NORMAL CHEST   EMPHYSEMATOUS CHEST

THESE SIMPLIFIED FIGURES SHOW THE EFFECT OF THE BALLOONING CHEST ON THE DIAPHRAGM. (BOTH FIGURES ARE AT THE SAME POINT IN THE BREATHING CYCLE.) NOTE HOW THE DIAPHRAGM IS STRETCHED SO THAT WHEN IT RELAXES AT EXHALATION, THE LUNG CANNOT FULLY COLLAPSE AND SQUEEZE OUT THE SPENT AIR.

Figure 3-1. A comparison of a normal chest with an emphysematous chest.

does. That is, your "functional residual capacity" is much greater than that of a normal person. The following example will clarify this further.

In a normal set of lungs, when you exhale, you will have about 2 quarts of air still remaining in your lungs. When an emphysema victim exhales, he normally has about 4 quarts left (for the sake of this example). Now, if the normal person and the victim of emphysema both inhale the same amount of air in a breath, say half a quart, you can see the difference in the result as follows:

The normal person is adding ½ quart of air to 2 quarts of air in the lungs. *The emphysema victim is adding ½ quart of air to 4 quarts of air.* The difference is what we might call "dilution." The effect of the fresh air in the normal lung is about twice the effect of the fresh air in the emphysematous lung. The same thing of course applies to exhaling to expel carbon dioxide.

The carbon dioxide or waste gas concentration in your lungs works with the message system of your breathing mechanism, so that you have the sensation of drowning or breathlessness to an even greater degree because of dilution.

As the condition of emphysema becomes more acute, you suffer more and more from an "out of breath" feeling caused by this dilution condition. To illustrate, we might consider an example of bathing. Normally, a person wishing to bathe, fills the tub full, gets in, bathes, and then releases all of the water. Now consider a condition where, when you start to bathe, the tub is already half full of the water from your last bath. Now you *add* fresh water to fill the tub full, bathe, and drain out half the water, saving the other half until your next bath. This murky kind of illustration serves to show the condition in your lungs each time you take a breath. You simply dilute the "dirty" or spent air with new air.

We have learned how the efficiency of your lungs has been reduced by the destruction of much gas-exchange-membrane area. The effect of this loss of area is also accentuated by dilution caused by the enlargement of the lungs.

Sufferers from chronic and advanced emphysema (referred to as lungers) are also always suffering from some level of infection. This infection, be it ever so small, continues to destroy small portions of vital lung tissue. Mucus and pus get into the openings of the small sacs (alveoli), which are actually the active or working parts of your lungs. This further reduces the vital capacity of the lungs by making it impossible for air to enter these air sacs.

As the emphysematous lung enlarges and expands because of coughing and gasping, these activities actually produce a breakup of the lung tissues. Often pieces of tissue will become isolated within the lung. Then as you breathe, the air pressure within the lung pushes or mashes them together with more force than the weak muscles can expend to open them. These "islands" of lung tissue become inactive by being isolated.

The various conditions which result in emphysema are summarized in the following:

1. *The rib cage becomes enlarged and loses its elasticity and mobility.*

2. *The diaphragm is stretched, and thus cannot close the lungs as far as the normal lung, due to the ballooning of the chest.*

3. *The air sacs are torn and fused by coughing.*

4. *The useful lung tissue surface area is greatly*

reduced by scar tissue produced by healing
of sores caused by infection.

5. *The cleaning mechanism of the lungs is damaged so that the mucus, dirt, and germs are
not moved up and out in the normal manner.*

6. *The elastic, rubber-like quality of the lung
muscle tissues is weakened, so that exhaling
becomes slower and labored.*

7. *The individual air sacs are often filled with
mucus.*

8. *Irritations cause the lung tubes to constrict
or contract, so that it is more difficult to eject
the mucus produced.*

9. *The lung has a reduced resistance to disease
and is easily infected by bacteria and viruses.*

10. *The lung is enlarged so that it holds more air,
and one suffers dilution effect.*

11. *The necessity for coughing is increased because of increased mucus load and reduced
efficiency of the natural lung cleaning mechanisms.*

So there you have it. Your condition snowballs—the worse
you become, the faster you become worse—*unless* you set
about to do everything within your power, with the help
of your good doctor, to prevent infections. Eat properly,
rest frequently, and live a life which is quietly, yet firmly,
molded to fit the capacity of your body.

There is no condition that is more demanding than
emphysema. As the condition becomes more advanced, the

victim finds himself faced with breathing difficulties 24 hours per day. It is relatively easy to breathe in (inhale), but exhaling becomes slower and more difficult. This, of course, is because the rubber-like elastic properties of the lungs do not act to close the lung, to squeeze out the air. As infection in the lungs becomes a common thing, the patient is almost constantly trying to eliminate mucus and phlegm. This is especially true on awaking in the morning, because the lungs have had several hours in which to produce pus and mucus without any elimination. Chronic lungers have at least one period of severe duress and suffering each day, and that is about one hour after awaking when the night's deposits are coughed up and spat out.

Some sufferers of emphysema feel that their problem is one of breathing in or inhaling, because their difficulty is one of getting enough air into the lungs. It is true that the sensation certainly is one of not being able to get enough air, but in reality, *the real trouble is not being able to exhale with sufficient vigor.* The chapters in this book discussing breathing exercises and the lungs will assist you to understand what really happens inside you.

The advanced emphysema sufferer can almost always be identified by his barrel chest. My chest is deeper or thicker than it is wide. Because of this chest expansion, it even becomes difficult to fit clothes properly, and it is almost always necessary to alter a suit to fit the enlarged, distorted chest.

Most emphysema sufferers I have known have a tendency to be thin, underweight, and have a stiff, upright walk with the shoulders held high and the back humped due to chest distortion. Being thin is certainly a blessing for one who is so short of oxygen, because you do not require so much oxygen to feed heavy tissues. However, with this thin underweight condition your ability to withstand long periods of illness and infection are greatly reduced. Therefore, you must take care of your body with a very strict set of rules.

The emphysema victim is always "tired." There just is no vitality left. It is uncomfortable to stand upright. You can often recognize an emphysema victim by the position he assumes when standing. Two favorite stances are shown in Figure 3-2. The most comfortable standing position is one where the emphysema victim can lean on his elbows which are supported by a bench or shelf of proper height. This seems to take a load off the diaphragm area. The other position is similar except that the arms are extended and the victim rests his hands on table or bench to take some of the weight off the midsection.

The midsection of the body is so "blown up" that X rays penetrate differently than they do normal bodies. Therefore, your doctor may have some difficulty getting a good picture. Doctors tell me that the heart is heard much less distinctly in the emphysematous chest than in a normal chest because of the "insulating effect" of the ballooned lungs.

If while you are reading this book, you think of anyone who might have tendency toward shortness of breath, asthma, or other possible lung troubles, for that person's sake, advise him or her to see a doctor immediately. *Early diagnosis and treatment of such condition might avoid the advance stages of this ravaging disorder.* This point of early treatment and care cannot be overemphasized.

IF YOU HAVE ANY DOUBTS SEE YOUR DOCTOR NOW, AND NOT AFTER EMPHYSEMA IS A GRIM REALITY!

ONE OF THE FAVORITE STANDING POSITIONS OF THE EMPHYSEMA VICTIM.

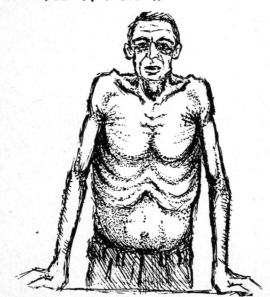

RESTING ON THE ARMS, WHILE STANDING, SEEMS TO RELIEVE BREATHING. THIS IS ALSO ANOTHER HELPFUL POSITION.

Figure 3-2.   The typical standing positions of an emphysema victim.

Summary of Chapter 3

1. Emphysema as a result of modern living habits; what aggravates emphysema in daily environment.

2. Emphysema is started by irritations of various types.

3. How the irritated lungs produce great quantities of mucus with serious consequences to health and life itself.

4. How vital lung tissue is destroyed; this tissue can never be restored.

5. Excessive coughing, triggered by irritants and mucus, causes the vicious spiraling cycle which ends in emphysema.

6. Shortness of breath is the first and foremost symptom of emphysema.

4

INFECTION—
PRIME ENEMY OF
EMPHYSEMA VICTIMS

Enemy #1 of the emphysema victim is infection. I suppose that it could be said that emphysema would not exist, at least in the form we know it today, if it were not for infection. If you could situate yourself in a place where there were no harmful germs, viruses, or bacteria, you might arrange to live a comfortable, enjoyable existence. *It is infection which makes the life of an emphysema sufferer seem to be a constant nightmare.* Your life will often seem to be a series of extended periods of infection, punctuated with small intervals of more or less normal existence.

The horrible thing about lung infection is the permanent damage. Your capacity for oxygen exchange is reduced to some degree by each attack. *The most important thing an emphysema victim can do to improve his health is to become an expert on infection, and how to fight it in his body.*

As we have learned, the lung's cleaning machinery becomes weakened by continuous irritation, and the cilia action becomes so sluggish that viruses, bacteria, and germs can penetrate deeper and deeper into the lungs, finally reaching the vital air sacs. These air sacs form the vital

51

link between your body and precious oxygen. Infection destroys this vital link, little by little.

In general, we observe that there are two types of infection which affect the lung. One we can term virus infection, which is almost always the first in line. The second we can term bacterial infection, which generally follows the virus infections.

Virus infections of the respiratory system are mostly called colds. Some are termed flu, Asian flu, or influenza. The virus is the smallest and "toughest bug" the medical profession continuously fights. Dozens of types have been identified which are associated with infections of the respiratory system. The virus is the "bug" that does the real damage to the lung tissue. These invaders are a veritable "wrecking crew." They simply rip the delicate surface of the lung passages and tissues and cause exposure of large areas like open sores. The virus infection is generally very violent and lasts only a relatively short time—maybe, as long as five days at the most. You can usually recognize the start of a virus infection by a sore throat or sensitive mucous membrane in the roof of the mouth.

When virus infection starts, your body declares war immediately. The adrenal gland emits certain hormones which mobilize the body's defenses. White blood cells, lymph cells, and antibodies are produced in great volumes. It is a fortunate thing that we do not have to depend on our medical scientists to protect us from virus infection. Medications are virtually 100 per cent ineffective against the virus. Millions of dollars are spent by Americans each year for so-called "cold cure" medicines. These medications have practically no effect on the virus army in our bodies, and we are forced to wait for our bodies to produce enough antibodies and lymph cells to overcome these invaders.

Many people think that a "shot" of penicillin will cure a

cold, but this is not true. Penicillin will help the body fight "secondary" infections, which almost always follow the virus. But against the prime invader, the virus, it is almost 100 per cent ineffective. The use of a proper diet and certain vitamins will assist the body to fight the virus, but medical science has not, as yet, found out how to kill them.

A recent breakthrough is a new drug called Symmetrel. This drug does not kill virus, but it does have a definite inhibiting effect on the Asian flu virus. The drug is so new that its effectiveness has not been thoroughly tested. But the concept of forming a barrier, which prevents viral penetration of the body cells, is certainly one which will be watched by the medical profession. It could be a real blessing to the emphysema victim.

As the virus army starts to work, the throat becomes sore due to mucous membrane sensitivity. Soon, the irritation travels down into the lung passages, and the lungs become hypersensitive. The body produces great floods of mucus, which are very corrosive, and the lung passages become actually raw, so to speak. Because of this condition, the coughing up of the mucus flood is quite painful. The mucus produced during the first stages of the virus attack is almost colorless.

Often I am able to recognize the first stages of a virus infection by the color in my face. When my body is battling an infection, the coloration just below my eyes, in the area of my upper cheeks, becomes extremely pink or even red. My face seems hot. In fact, I can often detect the virus attack by my facial coloration before I can feel it in my mouth or upper lungs, and before I start to eject much mucus. Then, the lower area of my chest, near the bottom of the rib cage, becomes sensitive, and there is a slight burning sensation in this area.

When the body has been able to conquer the first army

of "bugs," that is the virus, it is too bad that it cannot rest and start healing up the wounds. But, no such luck. A new army of invaders follows closely on the heels of the virus. This second army consists of bacteria of various types and kinds. The bacteria use the wounds left by the virus army as a way to enter the body tissues. These invaders, the bacteria, are attacked by the white corpuscles. The white corpuscles are killed by the millions as they make war on the invading bacteria, and the result is a large amount of material called pus, which is generally yellow in color.

It is this pus which is the enemy of the emphysema victim. It must be ejected and cleaned out of the lungs. The body produces mucus which dilutes this pus somewhat, and the resulting mixture is the product which causes the worst coughing and violent "fits" during deep lung infections. The material is extremely sticky, and it clings to the lung passages like glue.

Although it is an unpleasant subject, you must learn to examine your sputum, because *the severity of your lung infection is indicated by its color and texture*. A clear mucus with a few patches of yellow matter indicates the battle is going well for you. If the sputum is thick and almost totally yellow, the battle is very, very critical. If the sputum is brownish or greenish, watch out! You are losing the battle! Your doctor will definitely be interested in knowing the quality and quantity of your sputum. It is one way he can gage the severity of your infection and tell how your fight is progressing.

By this time your body is working with everything it can muster to defeat the army of invading foreigners. Fortunately, your doctor can aid your body to fight this secondary army of bacteria. If your doctor can start soon enough, he can administer antibiotics, which can be very effective in reducing the severity of the bacteria attack. (See Chapter 13 on medications.)

Antibiotics, however, have a very drastic effect on the bodily functions, and you should know how to offset them. Be sure to read the material in this book on vitamins, foods, and medications, because this information will assist and guide you through some of the problems caused by antibiotic intake. With the help of antibiotics, your body is able to finally rid the lungs of these bacteria, and you slowly return to normal. A bacteria infection can last three weeks, but most generally can be cleared up somewhat sooner.

Emphysema sufferers almost always have some infection in their lungs. By use of antibiotic treatments at intervals (as described in Chapter 13 on medications), you can help to keep your infection level quite low. The discharge from your lungs will be very slight. It takes a long time to heal the lungs, so do not expect miracles from antibiotics and drugs. However, you can continue to reduce the infection level in your lungs each month if you follow your doctor's advice and make an effort to assist your body in every way.

Infections are picked up by the emphysema victim very often and very easily. The so-called "common cold" is a disaster to a victim of emphysema. One of the most important things you can do is to start an intense program to avoid colds and also flu. The place to start is in your own family. All members of your family should consistently take Vitamin C, as this wonderful vitamin increases the resistance to colds. When one member does get a cold, isolate him or her in a separate room. Use disposable paper plates, drinking cups, and eating utensils for all meals. Do not allow that cold to spread to other family members and be passed back and forth all winter. If Johnny had small pox, an indulgent mother who would allow him to go

to school, a movie, or just out to play, would be repri-
manded, jailed, or stoned by her shocked and horrified
neighbors. But the child who has a cold from December
to May is a common occurrence, and he goes his way
spreading germs, infection, and also ruining his own germ-
laden body. In addition, he can be a catastrophe to any
person trying to maintain a perilous hold on life under the
handicap of a pulmonary malfunction, such as emphysema.

One of the finest things that I know to prevent the passing of the infections in the family group is the use of a
modern dishwashing machine. With the use of the powerful washing detergents and the high heat of these units,
your dishes really do come out sufficiently sterile. It is a
vast improvement over the old style, lukewarm dishwater
and soggy "tea towel," which often served to scatter the
germs throughout the whole family.

Another important thing to remember is the following:
ALWAYS USE DISPOSABLE PAPER TISSUE! THAT OLD-FASH-
IONED ELIZABETHAN CONVENIENCE—THE HANDKERCHIEF—IS
DEFINITELY OUT. THE ONLY REASON FOR SAVING SPUTUM IS
FOR LABORATORY CULTURE TEST PURPOSES, IN WHICH CASE,
AN APPROPRIATE VESSEL WILL BE PROVIDED FOR YOU TO USE.

If your friends or their children have colds, just avoid
them. Explain your situation and, if they are offended, they
are no friends of yours. A little child's cold is just as dangerous to you as an adult's cold. The "bugs" are just the
same. Avoid public meetings or gatherings when colds are
prevalent. Always get your "flu shots" each fall to help prevent influenza or, at least, to make the case lighter.

You should learn to recognize an infection in its early
stages and take immediate strong action to squelch it. This
may mean massive doses of vitamins and antibiotics, and,
perhaps, staying in bed. Contact your doctor immediately!
Do not allow yourself to become completely helpless, and

then expect your poor harassed doctor to come up with a miracle.

During periods of high infection, I have often had sore or sensitive areas at the edges of my rib cage, just above my stomach. I believe this is partially due to inflammation of the tissues in the area of my lungs and diaphragm. A great deal of relief is obtained by using an ordinary heating pad. I have a reclining chair, which I use for resting, and I find that by simply placing the heating pad on my lower chest for 15 minutes to ½ hour, I am able to reduce the sensitivity in this area.

When infection strikes, you should immediately start taking all of the expectorants your doctor prescribes. (See the discussion on medications in Chapter 13.) If you do this, the mucus that you are going to produce will cough up more easily and with less violent effort. Therefore, *the use of expectorants is very important.*

When you are taking all these treatments and medications, your other organs, such as the kidneys, are working overtime. Hence, drink plenty of water and juices to *keep your liquid level high during infections.* One of the worst problems of the lung sufferer is the lack of sufficient moisture in the body.

The most important medicine for the emphysema patient with an infection is rest. Because of the problem of getting up the large volume of mucus after sleeping for a long period of time, I have found it best to regulate sleeping to relatively short periods of time, say five hours at one stretch being a maximum. If you establish the pattern of sleeping four to five hours, awaking, emptying out your lungs, and then returning to sleep again, your coughing and eliminating efforts will be a lot less.

I have learned that I should have sufficient pillows so that I can sit up in bed with my body resting in a sitting position. Upon waking, I first get on my slope board for about ½ hour or so to get the material drained from my lungs. Then, I sit up in bed and wait for the mucus to come, and I cough and eliminate it. The period of waking and the first couple of hours in the morning are the worst part of the day for the emphysema sufferer. You should do everything possible to take the strain off your heart and body in general during this period. No one who has not experienced it can quite understand the difficulties—morning miseries—of a chronic emphysema sufferer. (More detailed information on getting up in the morning is presented in Chapter 17.)

Regardless of all the medicines, the main load of fighting infection is still carried by the body's white blood cells, antibodies, and lymph glands. When suffering from an infectious attack, you should do everything possible to assist your body to win the fight in a hurry. One or two days spent in bed or, at least, resting at home may save much later sickness. If only the young and vigorous person knew of the strain he places on his body by over-stressing it during illness, there would be less suffering during middle age.

An emphysema victim's life is geared to infection! If you can avoid it, your life will be relatively free of trouble! If you learn to be vigorous in the treatment of *every* infection, you will reduce your misery. If you are sloppy about your health and living habits, you will suffer continuously, without much hope for improvement.

Have a long talk with your doctor. Ask him to give you all the advice possible in regard to, firstly, avoiding lung infections and, secondly, treating them. Nothing can be more important to your improvement.

If you make a real effort, you can do a lot toward overcoming Enemy #1, that is, infection. Don't wait until you are sick before doing something. Start before the bugs do!

Summary of Chapter 4

1. Infections are the #1 Enemy of emphysema victims; each attack creates scar tissue and permanently reduces lung capacity to sustain life.

2. Types of viral and bacterial infections; how to cope with them.

3. How sticky pus deposits cause excessive coughing; how to minimize them.

4. Why the emphysema sufferer must constantly examine his sputum; necessity of taking expectorants.

5. Measures the emphysema victim can take for protection from colds within his own family.

6. Healthful living habits the emphysema victim should particularly adopt.

5

EFFECTIVE
BREATHING
METHODS

The normal person is not conscious of breathing at all. Just as the heart beats automatically, the eye blinks without conscious effort and breathing goes on twenty-four hours per day.

Many people, today, do not get enough exercise in their daily activities and so develop sloppy breathing habits. Shallow, sloppy breathing may be one of the underlying causes of emphysema. If we are to improve our breathing, we must relearn how to breathe effectively, and how to do the best job of getting air into and out of the lungs. This involves much rigorous training.

We have already discussed how your damaged lungs are so enlarged that you cannot force or squeeze out the spent, used air. Therefore, you are compelled to use air which contains a lower percentage of oxygen. If we can train ourselves to breathe effectively, we can at least offset a portion of the distress we suffer because of the dilution condition.

All chronic "lungers" have periods of great duress, emergencies, and real coughing "fits" when it becomes almost impossible to have any "control" at all. At such times, one becomes guided by the natural instincts of survival and battles to get enough air. This gasping in an uncontrollable manner happens to every lunger, so do not think that this is a criticism. Such breathing rarely, if ever, accomplishes anything, and the experienced person will make every effort to gain control by concentrating on proper breathing technique and rhythm.

When you have one of these so-called coughing spasms, you always breathe with great gulps of air and with great rapidity. This is the trouble. You are breathing too fast. When this condition occurs, you must always make every effort to *slow down.* I know this is not easy because this condition occurs to all lungers, sometimes many times in one day.

The technique of deep breathing described herein can assist you somewhat to establish equilibrium. One thing you can do is to forcibly hold your breath for a short interval at the end of each inhalation. This will help you to slow down a little sooner.

In many instances doctors refer to this type of suffering as hyperventilation. Breathing with such great rapidity, in order to restore your oxygen balance, has reduced the carbon dioxide content of your blood to some extent. This has the effect of causing your heart to beat faster. You develop a trembling feeling and, sometimes, you may get light-headed. These sensations are certainly not pleasant and create a great fear in the mind of the emphysema victim. You must force yourself to start breathing slower in order to establish a proper carbon dioxide to oxygen balance in your body.

Breathing involves muscles, and we all know that developing muscles requires exercise. Exercise requires effort, effort requires strength, and strength requires oxygen. People without good lungs are often hard put to get enough oxygen to exist, let alone exercise. So, exercise is not easy, but you must make a great effort if you wish to improve.

One of the simplest and most effective breathing exercises is called, by clinical specialists, "deep exhaustive breathing." We shall simply call this exercise "deep breathing." To do this exercise, take a normal breath and, then, breathe out slowly through your "pursed" lips. Your lips should be held in a position similar to that which you use to make a low whistle. Force the air out in a slow continuous stream making every effort to squeeze out just as much air as you possibly can. Strain a little! Take another breath and repeat, trying to once again squeeze out ALL THE AIR POSSIBLE! Strain a little harder!

After you do this exercise a few times, you will find that you get NOTICEABLE relief. You will feel like someone has added a lot of new capacity to your lungs. The object is not to take a deep breath, but to empty the lungs as completely as possible each time. If you blow the air out through your lips, as described, in a slow continuous stream, you can empty your lungs much more completely than if you breathe through your nose or with your mouth wide open. You should give this exercise a great deal of concentration, especially while learning what it feels like to really empty your lungs. Of course you will want to avoid overtaxing yourself, and you will want to do all breathing exercises when you are at your best. The object is not to breathe fast, but to breathe thoroughly.

This deep breathing exercise will strengthen the muscles of your lung tissues which squeeze the lungs closed at the end of each breathing cycle. Do the exercise several times a day for a period of five minutes or more. It can be done while standing, sitting, or lying down. Also, it is good to do the exercise in various positions as, then, different muscles are developed. Keep in mind that this exercise must be performed daily to get the maximum benefit.

When you are "deep breathing," clasp your hands behind your head with your elbows extended outward, as illustrated in Figure 5-1. This position will promote flexibility in your rib cage. One of the important things we want to do is to increase or, at least, keep any elasticity that we may have left in our rib action as it is a good part of the normal breathing process.

Do not expect these exercises to cause improvement in a few days or weeks. Remember that it took *years* to get your lungs in bad shape. However, I know from personal experience that you can definitely improve your breathing ability through the years if you *continue* to follow these exercises. Improvement will be painfully slow, but if you will keep trying, the results will be more than gratifying.

When doing "deep breathing," place your hands just below your ribs, pressing inward and upward to assist in getting your lungs really empty a few times. This exertion of pressure will certainly help to get the emptying effect, but it will not help to develop muscles. Therefore, do not use it all the time as you must *make your muscles learn to do the work.*

Another exercise can be done by lying on your back, on the floor, and placing a five pound sack of sugar on your stomach, just below the ribs. Practice deep breathing as described in the previous paragraphs. Try to completely empty your lungs each time. Strain a little! This added weight on your stomach will help you to develop breathing muscles more rapidly.

Still another breathing exercise can be practiced while you are doing "postural drainage" on your slope board. While you are lying on your slope board with your head lower than your feet, some of the weight of your stomach and intestines is pressing on your diaphragm area, at the lower end of your lungs. If you practice deep breathing in

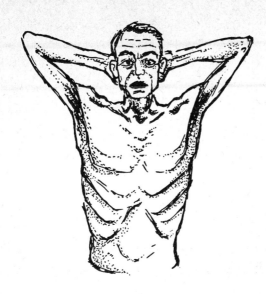

BREATHING WITH HANDS PLACED BEHIND
HEAD AND ELBOWS EXTENDED OUTWARD
HELPS TO PROMOTE RIB CAGE FLEXIBILITY.

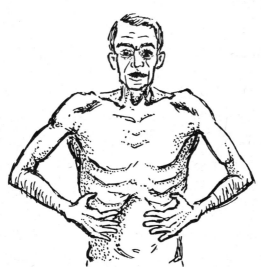

WHEN DOING DEEP-BREATHING EXERCISES,
YOU CAN HELP TO EMPTY YOUR LUNGS
BY PRESSING INWARD AND UPWARD,
JUST BELOW YOUR RIB CAGE

Figure 5-1. Deep breathing postures.

this position, the weight of your stomach and intestines assists you to empty your lungs. You are also forced to lift them as you inhale. Thus, you are developing your breathing muscles in both directions, so to speak.

At times, when I have had enough vitality, I have actually stood on my head, really on my neck and shoulders, by lying on my back and climbing up the wall with my feet, with some assistance. In this position the trunk of my body is almost vertical, and my legs are propped against the wall. This position puts most of the weight of my stomach and organs on my diaphragm. Breathing in this position is very helpful to the muscular development of the breathing system.

This exercise may be a bit rigorous for you at the present time, but keep in mind that anytime you can use gravity to lift your organs with your diaphragm, you are taking advantage of a wonderful opportunity to develop, in a natural way, your much needed breathing capacity. (See Figure 5-2.)

While I was getting control of infection in my lungs, which was a ten year program, I tried out many mechanical aids that I thought might increase my ability to breathe. One of the really successful things that my wife and I designed and made was an "emphysema belt." This belt helps to overcome the difficulty of emptying your lungs by pressing just below the rib cage. It has the same effect as if you were to place your hands at the bottom of your rib cage and press gently, but firmly, inward and upward as you exhaled.

The "emphysema belt" we made was the result of many trials and arrangements. The final belt consisted essentially of a heavy band of cloth and elastic which was supported from the shoulders by straps (similar to a woman's brassiere). The cloth band was, roughly, 6 to 8 inches wide and

GRAVITY ASSISTS EMPHYSEMA VICTIMS TO BREATHE IN AN UPSIDE-DOWN POSITION BECAUSE THE WEIGHT OF THE STOMACH HELPS TO COLLAPSE THE LUNGS.

BREATHING MUSCLES ARE STRENGTHENED BY INHALING AND EXHALING WITH A WEIGHT RESTING ON YOUR MIDRIFF.

Figure 5-2. Gravity aids breathing.

crossed the front, about one-half on the rib cage and the other one-half off and below the rib cage. Elastic bands were attached to the cloth in back, so that the band applied gentle pressure on the lower front rib cage and diaphragm area. We tried numerous closers with little success, as the garment had to be something which could be donned without the aid of a regiment. The problem of snaps, hooks, etc., was solved by using a nylon press closer. Perhaps you would like to try a zipper instead. We found that the elastic should not be stiff, and the most satisfactory belt applied very little gentle pressure. Try your hand. You can probably improve upon this design, as illustrated in Figure 5-3, but it gives you something basic to work from.

I wore my emphysema belt only during the day for a period of about five years, sleeping without it. It assisted me greatly in my battle with infections in my lungs. I know

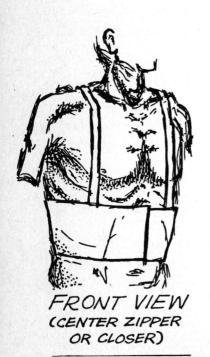

FRONT VIEW   BACK VIEW
(CENTER ZIPPER   (CENTER CROSSED STRAPS
   OR CLOSER)   AND ELASTIC BANDS)

Figure 5-3.   An "Emphysema Belt" you can make.

that this belt seems like a crutch and that one would think that the breathing muscles, which we are trying to develop, would become weaker. But, regardless of all these faults, I found that the belt helped a great deal, and I suggest you give one a trial.

Perhaps the "crutch" effect and the possibility of losing muscular development are more than offset by the extra amount of useful work and exercise you can perform while wearing the belt. Thus, in my opinion, the net effect is a positive one. You probably can gain muscular breathing strength while wearing your emphysema belt. In any event, I graduated from the use of the emphysema belt because I felt that I no longer needed that assistance. Now, I am not pretending to be another Charles Atlas, but today I can walk and perform the necessary things to be a useful citizen and hold down an office job.

Another observation regarding this belt can be made. Emphysematous chests seem to become more and more distorted, that is, barrel-shaped or ballooned. Although I have no proof, I believe that the use of this belt arrested the ballooning of my rib cage to some degree. As I mentioned earlier, the rib bones are surprisingly flexible, bending and contorting during the progress of emphysema. It stands to reason that a slight, but constant, pressure could cause the rib cage to keep its present or existing size.

The emphysema belt also helps in another way. The area near the lower rib cage becomes hyper-sensitive during certain periods of infection. When you walk after eating and drinking, you can actually feel the liquids "splashing" around in your stomach. This sensation is very annoying. The emphysema belt seems to assist in preventing this sensation or at least it makes it much less noticeable. While this was not the primary reason for my wearing the belt, I felt that it was a "bonus" one.

As you become accustomed to breathing exercises, you will find that you will be doing deep breathing without conscious effort or almost so anyway. When you do these things automatically, you are going to reap the real benefits. Make yourself develop good breathing habits! Do not be a shallow breather! If you force yourself hard enough and long enough, you will be pleased and surprised what service you can still get out of those old, burned out lungs.

Again I urge you to make an "emphysema belt." Do not try to make a finished product. Rather, pin and baste up something, and give it a try. If you do get benefit, you can make a good one which will last.

Summary of Chapter 5

1. Why the emphysema victim must re-learn to breathe; complete programs set out.
2. How author literally "stood on his head" to help his breathing using force of gravity.
3. How an emphysema belt aids breathing: Complete instructions for making and using emphysema belt to best advantage.
4. Excessive gasping for breath must be minimized to prevent hyperventilation.
5. How hyperventilation is similar to oxygen starvation.
6. Consistent breathing exercises improve ventilation.
7. When you are under duress, *concentrate* on proper breathing methods. This is extremely important to relieve your distress.

6

OXYGEN—
HOW BEST
TO USE IT

The air we breathe is a colorless, odorless gas consisting of a mixture of several element gasses. About 20 per cent of the air is oxygen in the form of two atoms of oxygen joined to form molecules, which the chemist represents as O_2. Nitrogen constitutes approximately 75 per cent. It is called inert because it does not react with the human tissue under ordinary circumstances. Nitrogen simply dilutes the oxygen which we use. It travels in and out of our lungs without any effect. The remaining 5 per cent of the air consists of several gases, the principal one being carbon dioxide.

In the process of photosynthesis, which goes into the making of food for the world by the plant kingdom, carbon dioxide is the key chemical compound. In this process the plants also produce oxygen. How dependent we are on the plants! They produce the food we eat, the oxygen we breathe, and also use up the carbon dioxide which we discharge.

Oxygen is the gas which supplies each and every living cell in your body. The blood transfers this oxygen from the lungs to the cells. So, finally, the real problem of every living person is that of a sufficient oxygen supply. Sufficient oxygen is the "name of the game" for the emphysema victim. The purpose of this chapter is to discuss emergency oxygen supplies which can be used by the emphysema victim in his own home.

Opinions vary regarding the benefits of increased oxygen content of air breathed by emphysema victims. We have learned that even though the amount of oxygen is increased, we cannot increase the volume of air we breathe in and out (our ventilation). Therefore, we cannot get rid of any more carbon dioxide. Also, we know that the lungs of the emphysema patient are so damaged that the area of useful tissue is extremely limited. Some authorities feel that this fact makes additional oxygen concentration almost useless. Regardless of opinions, if there is any chance that oxygen will help you in any way during those emergencies which all emphysema victims experience, please don't take a chance. Modern technology has made bottled oxygen so common that it can be purchased almost everywhere.

I have had an emergency oxygen supply at my bedside and in my car for the last ten years. I have used oxygen innumerable times when I felt that choking, gasping sensation of oxygen starvation associated with the coughing spasms of emphysema and its related infections. If it did not help my breathing, maybe it reduced the strain on my heart just a little bit. If it did not help my heart or lungs, perhaps it was a good psychological aid. Whatever the reason, whatever the help, I certainly recommend that every chronic emphysema victim have a source of emergency oxygen available at all times. It helps!

When you breathe oxygen during an emergency, the relief will not be as pronounced as you might expect. Primarily, I have found that this is true because when you are in a state of stress, you are almost always "panting"; that is, breathing extremely short puffs of air in and out, seldom getting enough oxygen into your lungs to do much good. If you can force yourself to once or twice exhale enough, you will begin to receive some real benefit. In my case my heart seems to slow down sooner, and I am able to reach equilibrium somewhat sooner. The proper breathing is of utmost importance in deriving benefit from oxygen therapy. *You must get the oxygen into your lungs, before it can help you.*

Emergency oxygen is available in all size containers. Small, lightweight aluminum containers of emergency oxygen, sold under various trade names, may be obtained at most drug stores. These cylinders are approximately 14 to 18 inches long and about 3 inches in diameter. Each cylinder contains a sufficient oxygen supply for up to 20 minutes. I carry one of these cylinders in my car at all times and also have one in my suitcase or briefcase when I travel. I have used this type of emergency supply twice in very severe and, what seemed to be, critical circumstances, both times with satisfaction. If you do carry these cylinders, be sure to check from time to time to be sure they still contain oxygen. Once in a while you will get one that leaks, and in a few days you are without your emergency oxygen and don't know it—a super emergency.

Emergency oxygen can be used in many different ways. Most kits are provided with a face mask and straps or clasps to secure it in position. These masks are supposed to flood the mouth and nasal area with oxygen to provide for efficient use. Various clever, imaginative devices and valves have been added by inventive geniuses who have never been closer to oxygen starvation than a drawing board. No doubt, the oxygen mask is a medical necessity for treatment of an unconscious person who has succumbed to injury or accident. However, for the emphysema sufferer, the mask is mostly useless. When you are fighting for air, the last thing you want is a plastic bag over your head.

When you are under duress, you automatically become a mouth breather. If you have a tube with oxygen blowing from it in a gentle stream, you can use this very effectively to assist you. The best way is to turn the oxygen stream directly into your face so that you breathe it as you inhale. This is especially effective if you turn your face downward and let the oxygen stream in an upward direction. You will avoid all those straps, covers, and other apparatus. This method may not get a 100 per cent oxygen supply into your lungs, but it gets a high concentration there when you need it. It probably could be considered a waste of oxygen, but oxygen is not so expensive. Especially during emergencies, we do not think of this "saving."

Any medical supply house can furnish you with an oxygen regulator and moisturizer which will fit standard oxygen cylinders. This equipment is quite simple to use and your doctor will be glad to assist you with obtaining it. Procure enough plastic tubing to deliver the oxygen to your bed. Get a piece long enough, so that you have sufficient slack to move about freely.

When I started to use emergency oxygen, I obtained an oxygen regulator from an ordinary oxygen-acetylene welding outfit. The welding oxygen regulator is made up with gages in a unit, which fits the standard oxygen cylinder. You can buy one of these units for a few dollars. By connecting a piece of plastic or rubber hose, 6 inches long, you have a primitive, but basic, lifesaving setup. I still have and use the same regulator, and it has proved to work very satisfactorily for me.

I use oxygen supplied by a welding supply house. These "bottles" specify on the label that the oxygen is usable as medical oxygen. Remember that oxygen is oxygen. Don't be forced or fooled into paying high prices for so called "medical oxygen." Check with your doctor. He will assist you to save as much as you can.

The oxygen cylinder size I use is called a "Q" cylinder. The "Q" indicates the size. This particular cylinder is about 3¼ feet tall, 8 inches in diameter, and weighs 75 to 80 pounds. It can be handled quite easily around the home with a small wheeled dolly. The oxygen bottle is stored on end.

You can generally get your oxygen delivered by a local supplier, and you can arrange to pay a small-tank rental fee. A "Q" tank of oxygen costs me about $3.30. Various suppliers have different arrangements, but you will find them most cooperative if you explain your circumstances.

Place the tank on end near your bed, so that you can reach the valve without straining. Remove the large cap which protects the valve. This is done by screwing the cap off counterclockwise, just like opening any threaded bottle cap. When you examine the valve arrangement at the top of your oxygen cylinder, you will note a "wheel." DO NOT OPEN THIS VALVE WITHOUT THE REGULATOR ATTACHED. The oxygen in the cylinder is under extremely high pressure, that is, 2200 pounds per square inch when the cylinder is full. The oxygen pressure must be reduced and regulated to give you a constant supply of low pressure oxygen, which you will require to breathe. Below the valve wheel, you will note a threaded outlet protruding horizontally. To this threaded outlet, you must connect your regulator. The regulator has a hexagon nut threaded on the inside which fits the outlet on the cylinder. Grasp the regulator and center the hexagon connector nut on the threaded oxygen outlet. Start to screw the hexagon nut on the outlet in a clockwise direction. Do not force the threads or get them "cocked."

When properly started, the hexagon nut can be run up by the fingers until the threads of the outlet are almost covered. Now take a CLEAN wrench and tighten the nut firmly. A 12 inch, crescent type, adjustable wrench will do nicely. USE NO OIL OR LUBRICANT AT ANY TIME.

Now you can turn on the oxygen valve on the tank. Turn valve about ¼ turn. The first of the two pressure gages on your regulator should read about 2000 to 2200 pounds, indicating that your cylinder is "full." If you hear any hissing noises, you will know that the hexagon nut connecting the regulator to the cylinder is not tight enough. Turn off the valve and tighten the nut a little more snugly. After you have mastered the connection of the regulator to the cylinder, you can learn how to adjust the regulator. The regulator is adjusted by turning the tee handle at its center. As you turn the tee handle clockwise, that is, screw the handle into the regulator, the pressure will increase. Turn the handle on your regulator until you feel oxygen discharging from the regulator outlet. Now, reverse the tee handle and notice when the oxygen stops. Put your finger over the oxygen outlet and turn up your regulator until you have about 3 pounds of pressure (just a very small way on the regulator pressure dial). This is about what you will want to use as a maximum during oxygen therapy. Practice and play with your oxygen equipment until you can, literally, work it in the dark. Sometimes you will do just that! Each time you are through using your oxygen, you should shut off the tank valve. If you expect to use oxygen every few minutes for a short time, it is satisfactory to use the regulator as a valve, but the tank valve should be shut off after each use period. (See Figure 6-1 for equipment details.)

As you use your oxygen, you will note the tank pressure falling. When it gets to 200 pounds or so, you had better

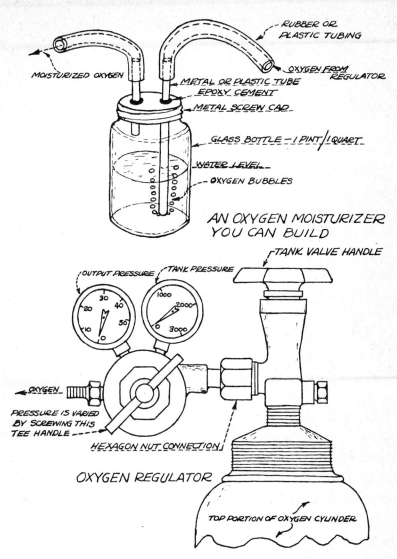

RUBBER OR PLASTIC TUBING

MOISTURIZED OXYGEN

OXYGEN FROM REGULATOR

METAL OR PLASTIC TUBE
EPOXY CEMENT
METAL SCREW CAP

GLASS BOTTLE – 1 PINT / 1 QUART

WATER LEVEL

OXYGEN BUBBLES

AN OXYGEN MOISTURIZER
YOU CAN BUILD

TANK VALVE HANDLE

OUTPUT PRESSURE

TANK PRESSURE

OXYGEN

PRESSURE IS VARIED
BY SCREWING THIS
TEE HANDLE

HEXAGON NUT CONNECTION

OXYGEN REGULATOR

TOP PORTION OF OXYGEN CYLINDER

Figure 6-1. Diagrams of oxygen equipment.

start to think about a new supply. Better give a little oxygen back than run out in the middle of the night!

Your oxygen regulator will prove to be a very reliable piece of equipment. Do not oil it—do not drop it—do not strain it. If there is a lot of dirt or dust where you store it, wrap it up in a plastic bag.

The tubing you use on the output end of your oxygen "rig" can be very light since it is under only slight pressure, at best. It can be spliced with adhesive tape or other household things. Take a little care and do a workmanlike job. It will last longer and serve you better.

One danger or, shall we say, disadvantage of using oxygen in this primitive way is the fact that the oxygen from the tank is absolutely dry. Breathing this dry gas tends to dry out the tissues and lung passages. However, you can make a simple bubbler-moisturizer, which will add a small amount of moisture to your oxygen supply. This can be made from a pint jar with a metal screw cap. A few pieces of plastic or metal tubing and a little Epoxy Cement is all you need. You can use ordinary tap water, but if you want perfectly sterile water, you can buy distilled water or "steam iron" water in your local market for a small sum. (Refer to Figure 6-1 for further details on this type of moisturizer.)

In using oxygen, several important things to remember regarding safety are the following:

1. *Do not allow children to play with your oxygen equipment.*

2. *Keep everything clean.*

3. *Do not use oil or grease on or around your equipment. This could result in a serious fire.*

4. *Do not smoke or have an open fire or flame*

near your oxygen equipment. Remember that oxygen promotes extremely rapid burning or combustion. Oxygen, itself, does not burn, but does make other things burn.

If you take ordinary precautions, you can use emergency oxygen safely. I have used hundreds of cylinders without any difficulty.

There have been many nights when I sat up for hours fighting for enough air to exist. Emergency oxygen certainly was a blessing to me. I used it for intervals of five minutes or so at various times to get me "over the hump," so to speak. I have never suffered any ill effects from the use of oxygen. However, your doctor will advise you on your use of oxygen in your home. The confidence you gain by having it available is worth the trouble, even if you never use it or if it really does no good at all! Keep your oxygen equipment. Even as you improve, you will be surprised at how often you will return to its use.

If at some time you feel oxygen might be required for an emergency, you can generally get aid from your local fire department. Most ambulance services also have oxygen equipment available for emergency use. Many lives are saved each year with the use of the green bottles.

Summary of Chapter 6

1. How oxygen maintains life; how it is distributed through the body; what to do for getting full benefits from oxygen intake in basic breathing.

2. Emergency supply of bottled oxygen is recommended for the emphysema victim; how to use bottled oxygen.

3. Carbon dioxide elimination, prime problem of emphysema sufferer, is not increased by taking in larger amounts of oxygen; how to handle oxygen emergencies.

4. Moisturizing is vital with intake of bottled oxygen; how to make and use a moisturizer.

5. Proper maintenance of oxygen equipment, how to buy oxygen most economically.

6. How to get oxygen into emphysematous lungs for maximum benefit.

7

POSTURAL DRAINAGE METHODS

To empty the lungs of foreign matter is the prime problem of the emphysema sufferer. Even the smallest pieces of mucus often cause nothing short of panic. The lung tissues are hyper-sensitive to any foreign matter. It is the constant effort to eliminate this foreign or unfriendly material that causes the violent coughing associated with emphysema. The interesting paradox is that *the cough is both your friend and enemy at the same time.* First, the cough is your friend because you must in some way eject the materials from your lungs in order to stay alive. Secondly, your cough is your enemy because the continuous violent coughing is the primary cause of the lung breakdown. Of course, what we want to finally accomplish is to back up a step and stop what is causing the cough. This is, first, the irritation and then, the infection. But in this consideration, we are attempting to determine if we can lessen the coughing effort.

As we have learned, the emphysematous chest has very little help from the natural cleaning machinery of the normal lungs. The mucus which is normally continuously swept up by the cilia (the miniature brooms that sweep the lungs) must be mainly ejected by some other means by the emphysema victim. This means, in almost all cases, coughing.

We all know that liquids run downhill because of gravity. With this simple fact doctors have developed a method of draining the lungs. This method is to let the liquids in the lungs run out or run downhill by placing the body in a position so that gravity can actually cause this to happen. Posture simply means the position of the body and hence, this method is known as "postural drainage."

Postural drainage is accomplished when the trunk of your body is so placed that your head is "downhill." The ordinary way to "drain" is to lie on a sloping surface with your head at the bottom. An effective slope is established for a person of normal height (5½ to 6 feet) when his feet are 2½ feet higher than his head. The tubes or passages of the upper lungs extend in all directions downward from the windpipe. In order to drain all of these tubes most effectively, it is necessary to lie in at least four positions. These are illustrated in Figure 7-1. The time required to get good results will vary with your condition, whether you have a lung infection or a cold, and the "stickiness" of the materials in your system. About 10 to 15 minutes in each position (back, left side, right side, stomach) should be sufficient.

It is not easy to lie down with your head lower than your feet. Your blood seems to rush to your head. You lose your equilibrium, breathing seems to be more difficult, and you may even become sick to your stomach. However, don't give up. Keep trying, because you will find that each day you will adjust a little more to this treatment. You will discover that it is a really effective way to get rid of the wastes in your lungs. Lying on your back will be the easiest position, and it might be well to use only this position during your first attempts at postural drainage. Start out with a very slight slope, perhaps with your head only 6 inches

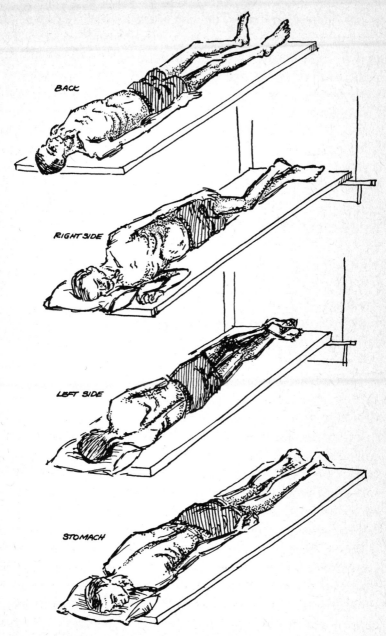

Figure 7-1. Four positions for postural drainage.

lower than your feet. You can increase the steepness of your position each day until your feet are 2 or more feet above your head. As you develop your tolerance to the position and confidence in your ability to lay upside down with comfort, you can start lying on your sides and finally on your stomach.

As you learn how postural drainage works for you it may become apparent that one position, such as right side or back, seems to give practically all of the benefits. If you find such to be true, you can adjust accordingly. You may also learn that one of the four positions is too difficult. Any position of postural drainage is effective. Therefore, do not abandon using this treatment because you find you can not use every position.

I find that I can get most effective drainage by lying on my back. Ordinarily, when I am using this treatment, I only use this position, unless the discharge is especially large. You will develop a good deal of judgment regarding your condition.

If your discharge is very slight, drainage may not be required at all during some periods. You should rest in a drainage position at least twice a day if you have infection or much discharge. I use postural drainage just after awaking and before the miseries start. In fact, I became so accustomed to this treatment that my wife would cover me, and I would sleep in this position for about 30 minutes or longer. I also take a treatment in the evening, a few hours before retiring.

The efficiency of your drainage will be increased by the use of one of the expectorants discussed in Chapter 13. The material flows much more easily. When you start to do this drainage, do not expect the mucus to run out like a river. Most of the time you will not experience any sensation of anything happening at all. However, do not be fooled! Although you may not get up anything for some time after you complete your drainage, this therapy does get the mucus to move upward and reduces the coughing effort a great deal. At times, some discharge will "run down," causing you to right yourself in order to gain control and regain your equilibrium. After the minor emergency, continue with your drainage.

You can find something to use for a simple slope board around almost any household. I have often used an ordinary door. A normal house door is about the right size and is certainly strong enough. A piece of plywood, 6 or 7 feet long and 2½ feet wide, is also a good board.

Since you will be using this board for a long time give a little thought to comfort and convenience. If possible set it up in a permanent place in your bedroom, even if it crowds things a bit. The upper end can be set in a windowsill or you can use a wooden box to support it. I obtained a small camp mattress, which I secured to the door with stout cords. This mattress was comfortable and gave me an anchor, so to speak, because there is a tendency to slide downhill all the time, unless there is something to prevent it. I had a small pillow for my head and, as I previously mentioned, my wife often covered me. Thus, I learned to sleep upside-down.

When you are away from home, you can improvise, using pillows, bedclothes, or something else to get your body in a sloping position. When you are learning to use your slope board, it will be necessary for you to have some assistance to get on the board and into the right position for reasonable comfort. As you progress, you will become quite adept in doing all these things by yourself.

There are other benefits derived from lying on your slope board. An emphysema patient can inhale almost as rapidly as a normal person, but when it comes to exhaling, that is

another story. Exhaling is painfully slow. After you learn
how to establish your equilibrium and gain full control of
your faculties, you will note that your exhaling process is
somewhat easier. This will be especially true while lying
on your back. This is because some of the weight of your
stomach and intestines is pressing down on your lungs,
helping you to empty them. Breathing in this position im-
proves tired and underdeveloped muscles. (See the discussion on breathing in Chapter 5.) You can use your drainage
period to also improve your breathing ability.

Once when I was in a clinic for some treatments, one of
the doctors put me on an X-ray table in order to use fluoroscope equipment to study my lung activity. (Fluoroscope is
the use of X-rays to see into the body, as opposed to taking
a picture and then looking at the picture.) The X-ray table
was arranged so that the doctor could, literally, stand me
on my head, thus putting all the weight of my lower organs
on my diaphragm and lungs. He remarked at the dramatic
effect this weight had on my lung activity. He estimated
my ventilation (breathing ability) was increased 60 per
cent or more. There is a good possibility that an emphysema patient could live much more comfortably upside-
down, as far as breathing is concerned. Of course this is not
practical, but it serves to illustrate in a forceful way how
important gravity can be to the functions of our body.

As in most of the treatments for emphysema, a great deal
of patience is required to use postural drainage effectively.
Do not give up or decide that it is too difficult. Perhaps
everyone cannot do postural drainage for one reason or
another, but most people can do it when they are convinced
that it will really help them. So keep trying. It is not easy,
but you will derive much benefit from your efforts.

Summary of Chapter 7

1. How the cough can be both a threat and a blessing to the emphysema victim.
2. Postural drainage explained to help eliminate pus and mucus from the lungs.
3. How postural drainage will reduce tiring cough efforts.
4. How to set up a slope board for postural drainage.
5. The four positions to take for effective postural drainage.
6. Various benefits of the slope board technique other than for postural drainage.

8

POSITIVE PRESSURE
BREATHING APPARATUS

Almost everyone has heard of the *iron lung*. It is a machine devised to make it possible for patients with paralyzed chests to breathe. These patients are usually victims of polio. The iron lung has challenged the imagination of many people and yet, another breathing machine, the positive pressure breathing machine, while not so well known today, is probably many times more important in the field of lung therapy.

Both the iron lung and the positive pressure breather work to get air into and out of damaged lungs. The iron lung works by applying a vacuum to the outside of the body, which is encased in a "can," so to speak. The positive pressure breathing apparatus works by blowing air under slight pressure into the lungs through the mouth and/or nose.

We all know the modern method of artificial respiration, which is called mouth-to-mouth resuscitation. To practice this, one person simply blows air into the lungs of another person through the mouth. This could be called positive pressure breathing which is "man-powered."

The positive pressure breathing apparatus accomplishes the same thing as mouth-to-mouth resuscitation, except that the pressure for blowing is supplied from a tank of air or a compressor, instead of another pair of lungs. The apparatus helps you to breathe by applying air at a slight pressure to your lungs each time you inhale. The machine is so designed that a sensing valve follows your desired breathing speed and rhythm.

The simplest type of positive pressure breathing apparatus ends in a tube, which is held in the mouth. (The nose can be held for a little while until one learns to control the breathing technique.) When you start to inhale, you simply breathe using the tube as a source of air. When you start to inhale, air under slight pressure "follows" your breathing until your lungs are "full." The sensing valve, which regulates the flow of air, is controlled by your demand. If you breathe fast, the air follows fast; if you breathe slowly, it follows slowly; if you breathe deep, it follows this pattern; if you breathe shallow, it also "breathes" shallow. When your inhaling is complete, you simply exhale through the same tube. You are *helped* to breathe by the slight pressure of the air, which is supplied by the machine. The pressure of this air is very small, approximately 15 centimeters of water or about ¼ pound per square inch. The flow of air is so controlled that it adapts itself to the patient, not to the machine.

This ability to automatically follow the patient's flow requirement allows the valve to ventilate through very restricted and congested breathing passages in the lungs and also render adequate ventilation to less restricted and more voluminous breathing passages. You are assisted in your breathing by inflating your lungs during inhalation under safe controlled pressure. Breathing can be at a rate which is best for the individual patient, because the machine does not cycle automatically. The breathing cycle is controlled entirely by the demand of the patient. This positive pressure accomplishes wonderful results, especially during periods of high infection.

The use of the machine is a pleasant sensation and certainly nothing to fear by anyone, sick or well.

The positive pressure machine also has another feature which is of vital interest to emphysema victims. The machine is equipped with a "fog-maker," which supplies moisture to the air that is inhaled. The moisture is supplied by a "nebulizer" (cloud-maker), which produces an extremely fine water mist. This mist enters the air stream as it is inhaled. The addition of moisture to thin down the stiff, glue-like mucus and pus is highly desirable in the treatment of infected lungs of emphysema patients. I found that it helped me get through some very serious lung infections which reduced coughing effort.

The moisture is introduced in a very positive way. There are no chemicals or reactions, just water put right where it is needed most. The water used in the nebulizer is a slightly salty solution which matches the salinity of the body. The solution is called a normal salt solution by doctors and druggists and is available upon prescription from a doctor for use in the positive pressure breathing apparatus.

Sometimes, when the mucus deposits become especially stubborn to move, doctors will use a "1½ or 2 normal salt solution" in the nebulizer of the positive pressure breathing apparatus. The increase in salt in the water causes the lungs to draw moisture from the tissues around them (to dilute the salt). Thus, the moisture in the lung is greatly increased. The effect is very definite and happens immediately. There is no pain or other sensation, except a slight salty taste in the mouth from the extra salt in the lung mucus which enters the mouth. Your doctor may want to use this to help you through some real tough spots. This movement of water into the lungs is a simple demonstration of a process known as osmosis. Less saturated solutions always move through a membrane to dilute solutions of higher saturation.

In normal, everyday use, treatments with the positive pressure breathing apparatus are given at specific intervals, such as two, three, or four times a day for periods of 10 to 20 minutes.

The apparatus is so designed that there are adjustments which can be made to accommodate each patient. The main adjustment, and the only one which is really critical for ordinary use, is the cut-off pressure or the maximum pressure which reaches your lungs at the end of the inhalation cycle. This is usually set quite low when you are getting the feel of the machine (approximately 5 centimeters of water), and gradually increased by your doctor to about 15 centimeters of water pressure maximum. The apparatus has a dial or meter on it so that the patient can observe the pressure at all times during the treatment.

The treatments are taken while sitting in a chair. The patient is generally advised to exhale all the air possible at each breath and to breathe deeply in order to extend the lungs to maximum inflation at each breath. Your doctor will train you to use the machine for your particular problem.

Sometimes the doctors will use one of the bronchial dilators in the water of the nebulizer on the breathing unit. However, since I have never experienced this, I can not report on results.

The positive pressure breathing apparatus works from pressure supplied from bottled air, oxygen, or a compressor. The units that work from oxygen pressure deliver ordinary air consisting of 20 per cent oxygen and 80 per cent nitrogen to the patient. However, some of the oxygen driven units have a control which allows for increase in the oxygen content of the air delivered. Therefore, the patient can breathe pure oxygen if required.

The compressor units work from ordinary household electrical energy and are probably more portable than the oxygen units which must have a supply from a tank.

There are at least two brands of positive pressure breathing apparatus available, and I used both of them extensively. I found both units equally satisfactory, and I believe either would last indefinitely with a little attention and care. In most areas you can rent this apparatus with a doctor's prescription. In large metropolitan areas there are services which check and service positive pressure breathing apparatus for hospitals and clinics. If such a service is available, your doctor can arrange for the service and adjustment of a rental unit while it is in your own home. I rented such a unit for a few months and found these services to be quite satisfactory. I would suggest that you first ask your doctor to arrange a trial series of treatments in a local hospital or clinic. If this seems to help you, then you should consider renting such a unit.

I have now purchased my own unit and keep it at my bedside. Normally, I use the unit twice a day for a period of about 12 minutes. When I get a serious infection, my doctor may ask me to increase the frequency of the treatments to four times a day.

My wife buys the normal saline solution (with a prescription) at the local drug store. The nebulizer is cleaned and filled, using a hypodermic syringe to handle the sterile salt solution.

The unit I purchased is driven from an oxygen bottle. Because I had been using oxygen at times to assist me in moments of high duress, I felt that the smaller the amount of equipment I had, the better. The positive pressure machine that I personally use is equipped with the oxygen dilution control. However, I have never, even under great duress, used anything except a normal air ratio of 20 per cent oxygen to 80 per cent nitrogen. I use it with a "Q" bottle of oxygen because this bottle is portable, being about 3½ feet high and weighing approximately 70 to 80 pounds. It can be handled in the home with a small wheeled dolly without too much difficulty. It is also portable enough to be handled in a car if required. The positive pressure unit mounts right on the oxygen bottle and is supported by the bottle as it sits in a vertical position. A bottle of this size will last me about five to seven days. I purchase oxygen from a local welder's supply house. Oxygen is also sold by medical supply houses. However, I suggest you check carefully as to cost before you make many purchases. Check the label on any cylinder of oxygen. It will state in part, "For use by trained personnel for oxygen deficiency and resuscitation." In other words, it is not the address of the cylinder that determines what is inside of it. Any oxygen bottle so labeled is certainly safe wherever it is purchased.

The purchase of one of these positive pressure breathing units represents quite an investment. Some units cost a slight amount more than a good hearing aid but, in my opinion, air to breathe is more valuable than noise.

This apparatus has been of utmost value to me. I also am sure that having it available in my own home every day is one of the basic reasons why it has helped me so much.

The use of positive pressure breathing therapy is becoming more and more popular. The medical profession is learning just how valuable a tool this machine can be in the treatment of emphysema. Be sure your doctor considers this treatment for you. It is an aid to improvement, not a last resort.

Summary of Chapter 8

1. Positive pressure breathing methods and how they operate.

2. How salt water is used in a "nebulizer" in certain apparatus to help move stubborn masses of mucus by drawing moisture from surrounding body tissue.

3. Mechanical breathers are available for home use.

4. What type of oxygen to buy for use with mechanical apparatus.

5. Use of apparatus for breathing is a pleasant sensation; average length and number of daily applications discussed.

6. Have your doctor consider the use of apparatus described for your particular situation.

9

WORK AND
EXERCISE

Your body is always working. It must work to live. You work even when you sleep. When you are sitting quietly in a chair your heart is beating, your lungs are being opened and closed as you breathe, your stomach and intestines are carrying on digestion, and your eyes blink. Yes, literally hundreds of processes are taking place all the time. All these activities involve work or, as we shall say, the "consumption of energy."

In order to produce the energy required to accomplish the work of operating your body, you must have a constant supply of food and oxygen delivered to the cells which are performing the work. Your body takes on food at intervals in order to produce energy. This food energy is stored in the body in various ways so that the body can produce energy for quite a length of time without more food supply. Thus, food energy can be stored up. However, you cannot store up oxygen. You must feed your body this vital ingredient on a *demand basis.* You might say that you are on a "pay as you go" basis when it comes to breathing the necessary oxygen supply for your lungs. You cannot store it.

If you are sitting absolutely quiet, your breathing rate is such that just the sufficient amount of oxygen is supplied to carry on the basic bodily functions. We might say that this is the minimum basic oxygen demand of your body, because (in a waking condition) you are carrying on your minimum work load.

Now if you raise your arm, the work load on your body changes. The cells, which perform the work, signal the brain that food and oxygen supplies are needed in a hurry. The heart rate rises to pump the extra blood required to deliver the food and oxygen to the cells and to take away the products of combustion and the carbon dioxide produced by the expenditure of the extra energy. The breathing rate also increases to add the extra oxygen to the blood and to expel the extra carbon dioxide. Your breathing rate can be increased in two ways. You can either breathe slightly faster or you can breathe slightly deeper.

As you increase the rate of work you do, your heart and lungs work together to supply oxygen to the cells *as the work is done.* A well-trained and conditioned athlete can do a tremendous amount of work. In long distance running and gymnastic competitions great feats of work are performed. The athlete is said to get his "second wind," that is, his heart and respiratory system become geared to the high rate of energy demanded, and the body is able to carry on a sustained level of work load for long periods of time.

Regardless of the work load, the body cells must be fed with oxygen and food at a rate equal to the work performed. In the performance of work by an athlete, just what is the limiting factor? Why can't the athlete go faster? There are several things which might be the limiting factor. The heart may have reached its maximum pumping rate so that it cannot deliver any more oxygen and food to the cells. The active tissue area of the athlete's lungs may limit the transfer of oxygen and carbon dioxide to and from the blood. The breathing rate of the athlete may limit the amount of oxygen which can be delivered to the blood. So you see, the athlete too is limited, just as the emphysema victim is limited. The only difference is the WORK LOAD. This is what establishes your limit.

Both the normal person and the trained athlete have a very large latitude of work load capacity. It is very seldom that they will work to a maximum or limiting work load. In this regard we might write the following equation, which expresses the activity of most people with normal respiratory systems.

$$\text{RATE OF WORK} \longrightarrow \text{RATE OF OXYGEN SUPPLY}$$

When an emphysema victim does heavy or strenuous work, the body cells send out an urgent call for oxygen. Due to the limited lung capacity (either breathing rate or tissue area), the oxygen cannot be delivered as fast as it is used. At the same time, there is more carbon dioxide in the blood than the lungs can dissipate. When you are in this condition, we say you are suffering from "oxygen starvation." A feeling of breathless agony overtakes the victim. Breathing becomes urgent, gasping, the heart beats wildly, and panic overtakes the emphysema victim. This oxygen starvation is a most continuous thing with the emphysema sufferer, and you will want to learn how to regulate your work load to match your oxygen capacity. This will do much to eliminate oxygen starvation for you. To accomplish this, we must understand *work* and *rate of work*. We must learn what our body does when it works and when it works harder, and why. In other words we must rewrite the equation of work for the normal person so that it fits the one with emphysema. The equation for working should be the reverse of a normal person:

$$\text{RATE OF OXYGEN SUPPLY} \longrightarrow \text{RATE OF WORK}$$

In this discussion we are calling any movement of the

body *work*. The "work" we do may not be earning money or doing a specific job, as such, but the movement of anything which requires energy is technically "work."

Work is done when the force of gravity is overcome. Most of the work you do with your body is involved in overcoming the force of gravity. When you pick up an object which weighs one pound, raising it up one foot (12 inches), you have done one foot-pound of work. If you weigh 150 pounds, and you step up a one foot high step, so as to raise your body 12 inches, you have done 150 foot-pounds of work. If you raise your arm, you do work; if you raise your leg, you do work; if you are sitting and rise to a standing position, you do work. Any time you raise any part of your body, you do work.

Another way work is done is by acceleration. Acceleration means to make things go faster. If your automobile is going 30 miles per hour and you wish to increase its speed to 40, you press down on the accelerator. This increases the power to increase the speed. After the higher speed is reached, it takes a little more power to keep going at 40 miles per hour. The only difference is the increased friction and air resistance, and for our considerations, we can neglect air resistance.

In the case of the human body, consider acceleration as you swing your arm as you walk. As your arm swings forward it gains speed (accelerates) until it reaches about the center of the forward movement. Then it starts to slow down (decelerate) until it stops at the end of the forward motion. The acceleration and deceleration both require work. Because the speeds involved are so slow in most of the normal movements of the human body, the amount of work done in acceleration is relatively small. However, it is real, and you can see how speeds do increase your work load. So, when you swing your arm, you are doing work two ways. You are raising your arm's weight against gravity a small distance, and the work involves acceleration and deceleration.

The same acceleration and deceleration process is involved in almost all the motions you make with your body. When you speed up violently, such as jumping up or rising very rapidly from a sitting position, the acceleration energy required can be very great.

It is the *rate of doing work* which is important to the emphysema patient. It is the work rate we must always consider. The work rate of a man or a machine can be stated as the number of foot-pounds of work done in a length of time. We generally use foot-pounds per minute. If you were to lift an object weighing 1 pound from the floor to a 2 foot high table, you would do two foot-pounds of work. If you did this work 20 times a minute, you would do 40 foot-pounds of work per minute (2 foot-pounds $\times$ 20). In order to show how work rate applies to the human body, I have shown work rates of calisthenics (gymnastic exercises) performed by a trained athlete. Along with these activities, I have also tabulated and calculated some data on various activities you might do, such as rising from a sitting position, climbing stairs, raising your arm, and walking.

These gymnastic exercises were performed at near maximum rates. I have calculated and tabulated this information to demonstrate to you that things you are probably doing right today are really athletic accomplishments. You do these activities without thinking. Nevertheless, your *work rate* is often very comparable to a trained athlete's work rate when performing vigorous feats of violent exercise. Now, we know that you will not do these things, such as rising from a sitting position or climbing a few steps, for as long a period as an athlete would, *but* your *work load* is the same for that period in which you perform this intense work. So, in theory, your lungs, which must supply oxygen *on demand,* should be as good as the trained athlete. Interesting, isn't it? No wonder you may suffer from oxygen starvation.

The athlete used in the tests weighed 153 pounds. His maximum rate of performance for the various gymnastic exercises was timed. Then, the weights of the various portions of his body according to the illustration were approximated. The tabulated calculations are the rate of work based on foot-pounds developed to overcome gravity. I have not included any acceleration work, so the values are low. But all the work values are comparative. See Figure 9-1 for details of the exercises.

The following table of calculations is quite revealing. It demonstrates that you may be performing athletic feats with lame lungs, just like a track star running the mile with a crutch.

Work Activity	Weight Moved (pounds)	Vertical Distance Moved (inches)	Cycles (per minute)	Rate of Work (foot-pounds per minute)
Push ups	153	14	60	10,740
Chinning	153	24	36	11,016
Sit ups	93	13	54	5,424
Deep knee bending	129	18	60	11,610
Rising from sitting position *	129	14	60	9,056
Raising and lowering arm *	10	12	80	800
Brisk walking *	See discussion	—	130	1,164
Climbing stairs *	153	9	120	13,770

* An emphysema victim may sometimes do these activities at these rates. Result ⟶ Oxygen Starvation.

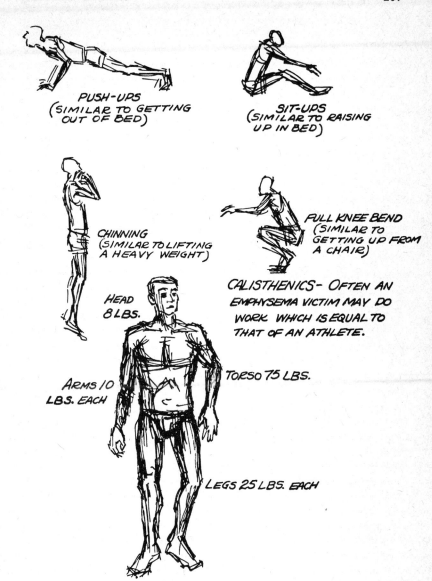

PUSH-UPS
(SIMILAR TO GETTING
OUT OF BED)

SIT-UPS
(SIMILAR TO RAISING
UP IN BED)

CHINNING
(SIMILAR TO LIFTING
A HEAVY WEIGHT)

FULL KNEE BEND
(SIMILAR TO
GETTING UP FROM
A CHAIR)

CALISTHENICS- OFTEN AN
EMPHYSEMA VICTIM MAY DO
WORK WHICH IS EQUAL TO
THAT OF AN ATHLETE.

HEAD
8 LBS.

TORSO 75 LBS.

ARMS 10
LBS. EACH

LEGS 25 LBS. EACH

ASSUMED BODY WEIGHT DISTRIBUTION USED FOR
COMPUTING WORK RATES. ATHLETE WEIGHS 153 LBS.

Figure 9-1. A comparison of athletic exercises with work
performed by an emphysema victim.

Because it is the most important work activity which you must do in order to carry on a normal existence, I will discuss the elements of walking in some detail.

When you walk, it is necessary for you to first take a step. You *lift* your leg a short distance, say 1 to 1½ inches, which involves work. Next, you push your leg forward, that is, you accelerate your leg to move it to take a step. At the same time, you probably swing your arm which involves work, as we have discussed previously. Due to the pivoting action of your hips, your body moves up and down about ⅛ to ½ inch. The distance you lift your body with each step depends on the length of your stride or steps. Short steps do not involve much lifting; longer steps cause more lifting. So now you can see how and why you get tired when you walk. You are actually lifting your body with every step.

The reason I am spending this time in discussing your body and work is to stimulate you to become a student of motion and work in all your personal activities. The emphysema victim has such a very limited energy capacity that he must learn how to use it properly to get the most work out of the limited oxygen supply. There is nothing more difficult to learn. You must make a concerted effort to pace yourself. Concentrate on such things as rising from a sitting position, climbing stairs (even a few steps), short (but mad) walking dashes. You must learn to slow down in these critical energy consuming activities. *You must learn to be deliberate in your motions*. Remember your equation.

$$\text{RATE OF OXYGEN SUPPLY} \longrightarrow \text{RATE OF WORK}$$

If you will concentrate on this one phase of your living, you will find you can accomplish many things that formerly seemed almost impossible. You will do things with relative ease. Oxygen starvation is very tricky. It is extremely difficult to convince yourself to go slow. Our minds just quite never get used to the fact that emphysema sufferers are not normal.

In your activities you should not try to keep pace with normal people. Do not be embarrassed by your inability. You will find that most people will be happy to cooperate if you are careful to explain your problem. You in turn should make every effort to avoid situations where a great demand will be placed upon you.

However, do not lock yourself in a room and decide you cannot associate in any activity. This is the worst thing you can do. Unless you are completely bedridden and under doctors orders to be absolutely quiet, you should do some exercise every day. Actually, a lunger's body goes to pieces and deteriorates because of lack of use as much as it does because of lack of oxygen. You must make every effort to keep up your body tone by exerting yourself somewhat every day. You will always feel tired, so do not always put things off until tomorrow. Do something today.

The primary daily exercise for the emphysema victim is walking. You do not have to go into the street or park. Walk in your room or in your home. Walking inside your home gives you advantages over trying to cover long distances. If you have two or three adjoining rooms you can "hike" there. You have the psychological advantage (which I find to be very great) of being able to sit down anytime you want to or have to. In this way you can really "push" yourself a little harder than you would if you were walking in the street. When walking inside, learn to count your steps. Open the window or door if weather permits. Do not be too easy on yourself. Try to increase the number of steps you walk each time. I used 100 steps as a minimum and added ten steps each "trip." This walking inside is so simple and beneficial. You can do it at work, at home, or most any place larger than a phone booth.

When you are doing your walking, try to relax your shoulders. Make every effort to let your arms hang loose, allowing your shoulders to "sag." This relaxing of your upper body structure will greatly assist in making your breathing more normal. Keep this in mind whenever you are standing or walking, because an emphysema victim is so "stiff" that normal lung functions are almost impossible.

When you are walking in the course of carrying on normal duties, always establish a pace to match your oxygen supply. If you must rest, do so before you are forced into an emergency. When you are forced to walk a long distance, there is a tendency to become apprehensive, worried, and anticipate trouble before it starts. In this condition you are not able to do as well as you could if you had a planned course of action. Count your steps. Decide to stop and "blow" (for example, every 500 steps). This will give you something to use as a series of minor goals. In any event, do not force yourself to become breathless before you really are.

You will use somewhat less energy if you walk with shorter steps, but not so short as to be jerky. Become conscious of your arm movements, keeping them to a minimum. When you walk, avoid talking, singing, or whistling, as all these activities require the expenditure of extra breath. The wind seems to make breathing very difficult. If forced to walk in the wind, hold your hands around your mouth as if you were going to shout. This reduces the "vacuum" effect created by the wind.

Your work load is increased tremendously when you are required to walk uphill. Even the smallest slope becomes a major challenge. Walking downhill is a delight! This is where deliberate and careful planning is required. I have often had someone assist me in walking uphill by standing behind me, placing his hands on my hips, and "pushing" me up the hill. I have found that if my helper is quite strong, I can "lay back," so to speak, and I can travel for a considerable distance with this assistance. This is something every emphysema victim should know as it might save him much trouble in case of an emergency. (See Figure 9-2.)

So far we have only talked about walking as an exercise for the emphysema sufferer. You must keep in mind that the smallest movement of any part of your body is exercise. Actually, flexing your fingers or toes, moving your hands, and bending your legs, even while lying down, will increase your body tone. Even standing without any appreciable moving at all puts some muscles to work. So, stand up, even with support if necessary, for periods of time. Any movement will assist to tone your body.

Because of your condition, it is easy to avoid doing little things. If you have a nurse, a good wife, or child, it is so

Figure 9-2. An emphysema victim can get assistance with a "push" when walking uphill.

easy to develop "lazy" habits, such as "hand me that,"
"bring me a drink," etc. Although it is painful, you should
make every effort to do as many little chores for yourself
as possible.

Exercise will be easier on an empty stomach, and you
get the same benefits as far as your body development is
concerned. Adjust your exercise period to the best part of
your day.

If you are forced to travel to higher altitudes, be very
careful with your oxygen balance. The capacity of your
work load will probably be reduced as you go higher.
Therefore, go slow until you find out what you can do.
Be especially careful after eating. A full stomach and a
high mountain can create a real emergency for an emphysema victim.

Most of us are faced with the problem of making a living. As an emphysema victim you will be forced to do
"office work." You may have to take some extra training
or correspondence school work to do this, but office jobs
are becoming more and more common in industry. This
fortunate circumstance is of benefit to lung patients. You
may not get the highest salary in the world, but you will
probably be much happier if you are gainfully employed.
This again takes desire, coupled with real effort, for accomplishment.

In summing up this discussion I want to again emphasize
the importance of becoming a student of motion. You can
greatly increase your usefulness and peace of mind by so
doing.

Summary of Chapter 9

1. Very little available oxygen can be stored in the body; how oxygen must be provided on a demand basis.

2. Emphysema victims suffer oxygen starvation; how to reduce this starvation by controlling work rate in their physical activities.

3. How the emphysema victim may follow the formula:

   RATE OF OXYGEN SUPPLY $\longrightarrow$ RATE OF WORK

   in order to maintain his best health and longevity.

4. Why the best exercise is walking; various methods of walking safely for health set out.

5. Why an emphysema victim should not attempt to "keep pace" with the persons not suffering from emphysema.

6. What exercises aside from walking can be taken to prevent undue physical deterioration.

10

HOW TO SELECT
THE BEST CLIMATE AND
GEOGRAPHIC LOCATION

Enough air and the right kind of air become the two most important things for the chronic emphysema victim. The climate in which you live can affect both the quality and quantity of the air you breathe. Thus, it becomes important to you as a lung patient to do what you can to improve your air supply.

The air you breathe can be hot, too hot, cold, too cold, dry, too dry, dusty, smoggy, filled with pollen, polluted with vegetable proteins, damp, too damp, thin, dense, etc. With these facts in mind, doctors for many years have been advising lung patients to move to higher and drier climates or to lower and cooler climates, etc., in the hope that the patient would get relief, and perhaps a cure, for their ailment. A change in climate can and often does effect a complete cure for children suffering from asthma, bronchitis, and other similar illnesses. For the emphysema victim we cannot hope for a cure by simply changing the climate. But, perhaps, we can make improvement simpler and make some of the stresses and strains a little lighter.

The first thing we will discuss is the density—"thickness" —of the air. At sea level the pressure of the air surrounding us is about 14½ pounds per square inch. This means that each square inch of our body, which is exposed to the air, has 14½ pounds of pressure on it. It is this air pressure which makes breathing possible. The air actually forces itself into our lungs as the muscles pull the lungs open. Now, if we move up a hill to an altitude of one thousand feet above sea level, we will find that the air pressure has gone down about ½ a pound. This means that each breath of air contains less oxygen than the same breath of air taken at sea level. The air is "thinner." As we go higher and higher, the pressure becomes less and less, and the air becomes thinner and thinner. Each breath of air contains less and less oxygen. This is the reason why airplanes have "pressurized cabins." By keeping the air pressure inside the cabin of the plane equal to the pressure at 5,000 feet, we are, in effect, breathing air at a density equal to being at an altitude of 5,000 feet, even though the plane may reach altitudes of 20,000 or 30,000 feet.

In the discussion on the lungs in Chapter 2, it was noted that, in most cases, breathing even pure oxygen does not necessarily increase the capacity of the body, because the lungs' ability to eliminate carbon dioxide is not increased in any way by additional oxygen. From the material presented in Chapter 3, we have learned that the limiting factor for the lungs may be the active tissue area left after repeated infectious attacks. Thus, you can see that, when it comes to the oxygen content of the air, it is difficult to establish just what the critical factor is.

In my own case, I find that I can live and breathe much more comfortably at or near sea level. Doctors in some cases may disagree with the reasoning, but I believe that every chronic lunger, if he has the opportunity, should try to keep to the lower altitude areas.

Another thing that I believe is important to include in my discussion is the dampness (humidity) of the air. When you boil water, the water turns into vapors which are "held" in the air, although you cannot see it. Hot air can hold more water vapor than cold air. This is the reason we have "dew" in the morning. Warm air, which has a large amount of moisture in it, becomes cooled during the night. Therefore, it cannot "hold" as much moisture and the water vapor is deposited in the form of dew. A cold glass "sweats" for the same reason. The air adjacent to the glass has been cooled below its "dew point."

The term, "relative humidity," is often used when weather reports are given on television and radio. Relative humidity is a measure of the amount of water vapor in the air. One hundred per cent humidity means that the air is "full," so to speak, and can hold no more water. Zero per cent means absolutely dry air.

As far as humidity is concerned, we know that one of the most necessary things for the comfort and improvement of the "lunger" is plenty of moisture in the lungs. Therefore, if other conditions of temperature are satisfactory, damp air or air with a relative humidity of from 60 to 80 per cent should give more comfort than dry air. Most emphysema victims are mouth breathers, and they dry out the tissues of their mouth and upper respiratory tracts very rapidly when the air is dry. In most instances, the emphysema victim is fortunate when it comes to humidity. It is relatively easy to add moisture to air with the things we have around the house, but it is relatively difficult to dry the air. In dry climates cooling in the home is often accomplished by "water coolers" or evaporative coolers. The evaporation of water into the air has the effect of cooling the air and raising the humidity, which is an automatic double assistance. Cooler, damper air, just what the doctor ordered, is the result.

In the winter or when cooling is not required, it is very simple to add moisture to the air by boiling water on the stove. The small electric vaporizers available in drug stores are too small to assist in adding much moisture. I find that the oils and medications offered with these units are absolutely useless to me and actually cause me more harm than good.

The air holds an amazing amount of moisture. However, it will probably be necessary to keep boiling water most of the time during cool, dry weather in order to add enough moisture. Remember all houses "leak," so the moist air is being lost to the outside through thousands of small openings. Just because the windows are sweating or are steamy, it does not mean that the air is full of moisture. Steamy windows indicate that the glass is cold due to outside temperature and that a layer of air near the glass has been cooled sufficiently to cause it to lose the moisture in it.

Of course, if the high humidity bothers you or causes breathing difficulties, reduce the amount of water you are adding. However, keep in mind that any amount you can add with comfort will be of great assistance.

The next thing to consider is temperature. The normal lung has an enormous capacity for heating or cooling the air breathed. Damaged lungs have lost some of this ability because of forced mouth breathing and loss of breathing action. Therefore, the emphysema victim is quite sensitive to the temperature of the air. Comfort of the human is related to the temperature-humidity ratio. Our bodies depend on evaporation of perspiration for cooling. Thus, when there is high humidity, the moisture on our skin does not evaporate as fast, and we lose our cooling ability. This effect is very pronounced during the summer months in many sections of the country.

Most emphysema victims I have known are really more sensitive to heat than they are to cold. They are especially sensitive to humid heat because the body has to struggle to maintain temperature control.

The evaporative cooler or water cooler is practically useless for home cooling when the humidity is very high. This is where the modern unit air conditioners are a real blessing. These units are relatively inexpensive to own and run dependably for many years. A small window unit will cool a portion of your house satisfactorily, and you can arrange to make the most effective use of such a unit. In the humid, hot areas of the country a small refrigerating-type air conditioner is practically a must for the emphysema sufferer.

Heating of some type is required in practically every area of the country. The thing to look for in a heating unit is air contamination, or I should say, the lack of it. The heat arrangement of any unit which consumes fuel, whether it is of the wood, coal, oil, or natural gas variety, must be vented to the outside. Wood and coal burning stoves or fire places are vented by their very natures. Emphysema victims should *definitely avoid* the use of oil, kerosene, or natural gas heaters which are not vented to the outside. The use of the so-called "suicide gas heater" must be avoided at all costs. I believe that a portion of my lung damage was caused by sleeping in a room that was heated by an unvented, radiant natural gas heater. These radiant heaters are furnished with clay-asbestos elements which are heated to incandescence, that is, to a white glowing heat, and are supposed to produce harmless products of water and carbon dioxide. But, such is not the case. Natural gas has many impurities in it that are not burned. The breathing of the products of these burners is slow death for anyone and for the emphysema victim practically legal murder. It is better to freeze to death! Use an electric heater, an electric blanket, or anything but an open gas heater. Avoid using the oven in a natural gas cooking stove as a heater! This is even worse than a radiant heater unit.

The ideal heat is of course electric heat which does not burn fuel. A satisfactory heat is a gas fired and vented gravity furnace, floor furnace or forced air heating system.

We have discussed air density, humidity, and temperature. In the world there are infinite combinations available. I have found the most satisfactory climate for emphysema is near the ocean (sea level), because the temperature ranges from a high of 85° F. to a low of 45° F., and the humidity is naturally high most of the time. I know that everyone with emphysema cannot move around, trying all the various climates. But, sometimes, if one has a choice, a good guide-line is a great help. We want to remember that climate does not cause infection. Infection is caused by viruses and bacteria which exist almost everywhere. However, some climates are much more conducive to colds and virus infections than others. If you have the choice, it is good to live in a place where colds are at a minimum.

Much of our country is covered with plants and grasses, which produce pollens, plant dusts, and vegetable proteins. Some of these natural plant dusts can be very annoying and corrosive to the hyper-sensitive lung tissue of the emphysema victim. If you live in an area where these dusts occur, you can now obtain electrostatic air filters for use in your home. These will do an effective job of removing them, and your doctor can probably direct you to the most satisfactory type. Some of the units work for only one room. Therefore, be sure to consider your sleeping room in your plans.

I once tried to use a small air purifier which had a small ultra-violet light source, an ozone generator, and a very small fan, which pushed a few cubic feet per minute through a little filter pad about 3 or 4 inches square. The sweet smell of ozone was soon in evidence in the room, but that was about all. This unit was supposed to be a great boon to hay fever victims, and I thought it might help me with my problems of dust and pollen in the air. The unit was useless, as far as I could determine, for emphysema therapy. Perhaps the ozone did kill bacteria and germs, and perhaps the ultra-violet light did tend to sterilize what small amount of air the fan did blow through the unit, but I was unable to detect any aid to my comfort, breathing and/or health.

Keep in mind that there is a difference between a purifier and a filter. A filter removes particulate matter from the air. This can include bacteria, virus, and germs.

I know that you have often seen a ray of sunshine passing through the air in your home, and you no doubt have been astounded at the great amount of dust and dirt which are shown up by that ray. Household dusts are often a very special enemy of the lunger. We live in a civilization of fibers. Everything produces dust; clothes, carpets, beds, drapes, packing materials, an endless list.

You should make every effort to keep the dust level in your home at a minimum. "Dusting," as such, does very little good. When the average cleaning job is done with such tools as a broom and a feather duster, all that is accomplished is that the dust, which was settled, is stirred up into the air again to settle somewhere else at a later date.

A vacuum cleaner and damp cloths and sponges will do a reasonably effective job of cleaning without doing too much "stirring." One thing that should be avoided is stirring up the dust in your room just before you go to bed. It is the habit of all homemakers to want to fluff-up the bed, and often they want to tidy and shake-out things just before bedtime. If these good people could only realize that they are placing a terrible amount of dust and dirt in suspension in the air just when the poor old lunger is going to start to breathe it! Clean up in the morning after the lung patient is out of that room and do nothing to disturb it at night unless you are forced to do so. LET SLEEPING DUST LIE! You cannot breathe dust that is on a table, just the dust that is in the air!

Another air pollutant which is quite common in the home is cooking fumes or odors. The emphysema victim is often so hyper-sensitive that the fumes from a piece of burnt toast are enough to set off a coughing spasm and cause much agony. The odors of frying foods are the worst, of course. Try to use a little judgment in cooking and be sure that your vent fan over your stove is working well. When cooking accidents happen, be sure to air out the house thoroughly and immediately.

No discussion would be complete without including "smog." Smog is smoke and fumes which are mostly by-products arising from the burning of hydrocarbons. These hydrocarbons or fossil fuels include coal, oil, fuel oil, natural gas, gasoline, and diesel fuels. Smog is produced by power plants, smelters, factories, automobiles, and trucks. Today, smog is so strong in the large cities of our country that it causes your eyes to water. In fact, one way the intensity of smog is measured is by eye irritation intensity. The city dweller is told to expect slight, medium, or severe eye irritation. Now, if the materials and fumes in the air are strong enough to make your eyes smart and water, don't you think they would be damaging to the delicate lung tissues of an emphysema sufferer?

Smog is very irritating to my lungs. When I am exposed to city smog for a couple of days, the mucus and discharge from my lungs increases, and I start to feel the irritation quite severely. I am surprised that doctors, according to the published reports I have read, are divided on the dangers of smog to health. My experience teaches that, if you have emphysema, you should avoid living in a smog area.

This short discussion has shown you how to control the climate in which you live to some degree. Also, I would suggest that you might like to obtain a thermometer and a humidity meter so that you can learn to observe the conditions of the climate in your home. This will help you make what corrections you can for your convenience and comfort to bring about better health for you.

Summary of Chapter 10

1. How climate and geographical location govern daily well-being of emphysema victim.
2. Lower altitudes with high humidity are desirable locations; benefits of oceanside locations.
3. Use of various devices to moisturize, cool and heat; how to control dust in living quarters.
4. Types of heating equipment to avoid.
5. Importance of avoiding smog areas; checking a location where respiratory infections are at a minimum.
6. Why environmental conditions should be checked on a daily basis.

11

FOOD AND GOOD EATING HABITS

The emphysema victim's chest and lungs are so enlarged that there simply does not seem to be enough room for everything inside the body cavity. The diaphragm is displaced downward, thus crowding the room ordinarily occupied by the stomach and intestines. When the stomach is empty this condition is not so noticeable. But, after a big meal, the lunger suffers much discomfort. I have often said and I have heard others also agree, "I could get along very well if I did not have to eat." Yes, eating becomes a real task to an advanced lunger, and it is so important to his improvement and general well-being that it is worthy of a few comments here.

The food we eat takes up room, crowding the lungs and reducing their air capacity. The digestive process is also adversely affected by the lack of sufficient oxygen. Consequently, after the food is consumed, the patient often suffers from indigestion and gas, which causes great pain and misery.

In considering eating, I shall divide the subject into the following parts:

1. How to eat.

2. What to eat.

3. When to eat.

I am not trying to recommend certain foods or develop scientific diets to help gain, lose, or control weight. Others, who are better qualified, have already covered these subjects very well. Rather, I am going to present material on what might be called the "mechanics of eating," with regard to the special requirements of the emphysema sufferer.

The victim of chronic lung disorder is almost always gasping for air. You get so used to doing this that you are not really conscious of it. This gasping is your enemy when it comes to eating and drinking. Each swallow you take may trap a bubble of air due to your gasping and this air, when swallowed, causes you to become bloated. Thus, you have an artificial gaseous condition even before indigestion, if any, takes place. You can learn to avoid swallowing much of this trapped air by being conscious of the trouble and swallowing with slow controlled motion. I know that, of the necessities of life, air is the most constantly demanded. But, you will find that you can control your breathing in regard to the chewing and swallowing of food and in the drinking of liquids. I have found this to be very helpful in avoiding some of the misery of eating. Swallowed air is normally cooler than the body. After it is swallowed, it heats to body temperature and expands as it is heated, as is normal with all gases. This further increases the discomfort. This swallowed trapped air is by far the most serious of your problems. You must concentrate on your chewing and swallowing habits to lessen the trapped gas. One thing you can try is to drink your liquids through a straw. This may assist to eliminate some of the gas trapping in liquids.

Sometimes, eating requires so much effort for the lung patient that it becomes a major task to do it. Do not feel that you are compelled to eat as rapidly as normal people do, if, indeed, it is normal to bolt one's food. Relax! Rest for small intervals. Give your body time to gain as much balance as possible.

Once in a while my system is in such a condition that forcing food into my body is a major operation. I just do not feel like eating. I am having an especially hard time breathing. I have pressure from gas or some other stuffed-up feeling. I have learned that under these conditions, it is better to not eat at that particular time, but to wait until the worst is over. Under no circumstances should you eat when you are angry, worried, or "worked-up" over some other problem, be it large or small. The emphysema patient must realize how important the emotions are to the proper use and digestion of food. If you have to eat when you are under emotional strain, it will probably do you more harm than good.

Perhaps one of the comforting things for the chronic lunger to know is that the stomach will digest an amazing variety of material. As noted from Adelle Davis' book *Let's Get Well,* the stomach, healthy or ulcerated, "processes impartially any material classified as edible." The investigators pointed out, however, that apprehension could cause the stomach to become inflamed before a food or drug was taken. This certainly is true of the victim of emphysema. Wives, nurses, families, please take note of the following:

DON'T UPSET THE EMPHYSEMA VICTIM BEFORE, DURING, OR AFTER HIS MEALS. IN FACT, JUST DON'T UPSET HIM!

The modern labor-saving, body-ruining foods which are bleached, canned, adulterated and emasculated, are short of the natural enzymes which aid in the digestive processes. The same property of food which enables it to be digested easily also enables it to spoil rapidly or turn rancid. Such a condition is not conducive to large or stable profits in the sale of foods. A person who must rely on small quantities of bulk will find it difficult to consume enough food to supply his starving tissues from the average supermarket. Therefore, I would recommend that you find a good health food store and become familiar with the really fine food that is available. Because anyone who has emphysema is under stress conditions a great part of the time from infection or emotional distress, it is important that he get the best possible food. There is not much room for the usual fillers here.

As your lung condition becomes more acute, you are forced to slow down, to do less work, and to use up less energy food each day. This means that your diet will have to be altered from that of a normal person's diet to include more body building materials and less energy producing materials.

Foods may all be classed under one of the general headings of proteins, carbohydrates, fats, vitamins, and minerals. The energy-producing foods, such as starches and sugars, are the carbohydrates. Now, this is not to say that you should stop eating bread, potatoes, and so on, but you should concentrate on eating a higher percentage of protein, such as meat, eggs, and cheese, etc. Frequent small meals are tolerated better than several large meals. You should consume as much liquid as possible, because you will find that you will require a great deal of moisture to keep your body working properly.

Avoid foods which you find are difficult to digest. A severe gas attack after eating a certain food may trigger apprehension that it will occur again. The fear may give you indigestion before the food is even eaten. If you cannot control your apprehension, give up that food!

Some of the foods which I try to avoid, especially in the evening, are ground beef, roasted nuts, raw onions, candy, and very rich desserts. There is no rule which will necessarily apply to you. You must find your own weaknesses and avoid them.

Seafoods are one group of foods that I rely on with most satisfying results. I find that fish, crabs, shrimp, clams, etc., give me little, if any, digestive trouble at any time. If you don't like fish, this isn't going to help you much.

As discussed previously, modern prepared foods are short of natural enzymes which aid in the digestive process. I have tried many types of health foods and special preparations in an effort to aid my eating problem, and I can recommend the following as giving me good results.

Milk

Most milk today is pasteurized and homogenized. The pasteurizing process destroys the natural milk enzymes, and the homogenizing process destroys most of the Vitamin A. This makes the acquisition of a certified raw milk very important. Certified milk is produced under controlled, clean conditions from special herds. The milk is tested for bacteria count and "certified" to be as safe as pasteurized milk for human consumption. The use of certified raw milk in my diet has helped immensely with my digestion problem. I consume about one quart of milk per day, frequently more rather than less. Milk is very high in proteins and minerals and is certainly an ideal food for emphysema victims. Don't think that you should take milk out of your diet because you think that it will cause mucus. The body does not produce mucus from milk any more than it does from many other foods.

Papaya

Papaya is a tropical fruit. It is the source of many enzymes which assist the stomach to digest food. The fruit has a melon-like flavor, and a small slice once a day will assist greatly with digestion. If this fruit proves to be too expensive or it is not available in your area in the raw state, it is now canned and is available in most markets. The canned fruit is a fine aid to digestion, but is not nearly so effective as the fresh fruit, as is usually the case. A papaya concentrate in pill form is available in health food stores, and I recommend these to the unfortunate victim of emphysema or any digestive disorder. This papaya pill is convenient to carry in pocket or briefcase and may be chewed or swallowed whole, with little fuss or bother. It will enable the sufferer to head off the frantic efforts of his stomach to cope with the delicacies with which we regularly insult it.

Yogurt

Antibiotics taken by mouth kill most all intestinal bacteria. In order to replace these vital bacteria, it is necessary to provide the body with yogurt or acidophilus milk. I personally prefer yogurt. Not only is it useful when you are taking antibiotics, but you should also use it often as an aid to digestion. There is nothing finer available. It is a natural milk product and a well-known health food, and it can be said to be the only predigested food that is almost universally available in dairy delivery services, markets, and health food stores. Yogurt will never give you indigestion and, if you eat a small portion with your meals, it will greatly aid digestion. Yogurt is quite sour. Therefore, you can mix a small portion of jam or fruit preserves with it to make it more palatable if you do not enjoy the tart taste. Yogurt can be made at home to save considerable expense. It seems to me that the homemade yogurt is more wholesome. However, this is a personal preference. You can obtain recipes for yogurt preparation at your health food store.

Water

Drinking water and plenty of it is so important that I have discussed it in Chapter 13 dealing with medications. However, it is mentioned here also because the importance of water cannot be overemphasized.

Oranges and Citrus Fruits

Under the heading of vitamins I have explained the importance of Vitamin C in the fight against infection. I again include the importance of eating citrus fruits each and every day.

Foods Containing the Vitamin B Complex

We have said nothing about the B vitamin group, and its special importance to you as a person who is getting along on a short supply of oxygen. I do wish that I could say that lemon cream pie and chocolate cake are indispensable in the diet of the victim of emphysema. However, some killjoy would probably tell you the truth anyway. They do not contain Vitamin B in any of its forms and, therefore, you can take them or leave them alone.

It is impossible to be well nourished and still be lacking in any of the vital food elements. I am not an expert on nutrition. However, there are some facts that I would like to call to your attention. We depend on the complex B group of vitamins for endurance, energy, and a sense of well-being. By energy we mean not only energy to move about and perform reasonable functions, but also the energy required by your body to perform such necessary and basic tasks as food digestion and waste elimination.

Because of their complex and interrelated action in your body, many experts on nutrition feel that trying to provide the Vitamin B requirements with only pills is dangerous and not very helpful. Since they are generously provided by such foods as liver, wheat germ, brewer's yeast, and yogurt, there is no reason to run this risk. If, perhaps, these are not now your favorite foods, they could be if you cultivate a taste for them. Use a little imagination in their preparation and know the advantages of their use. Learn to like them! You need all the help you can get! You are probably familiar with liver. However, if you have never used brewer's yeast, you should begin so in small amounts until your digestion is sufficiently improved to tolerate it easily. Not all brewer's yeast is delicious, but some of it is, especially so when mixed with apricot nectar and milk. It makes a drink that is high in nutrition and small in volume. Just what you need when under stress. You may find it very beneficial the first thing in the morning when you are worn out by your usual efforts at mucus elimination.

Now, we still have the problem of when to eat. A lung patient, of course, has his worst time in the morning. Therefore, eating is often not desirable or satisfying. In the morning I try to drink a glass of milk with a powdered food concentrate in it. Brewer's yeast combined with apricot juice is also very good. With this, I take my vitamin capsules and any other medication. If possible, I eat some fruit or drink some orange juice. Now, after your morning difficulties are over, you can develop some enthusiasm for food, preferably some good protein, such as eggs, meat, or fish. If you work, you will be forced into the customary three meals. But, in any event, try to eat your final meal as early as possible. In this way you can get your digestive processes well along before you retire. If you are forced to eat very late hold down the volume! A study of American eating habits indicates that over 60 per cent of all food consumed is eaten after 6 P.M. This is precisely the opposite of what is desirable for good health.

I consume coffee and tea in moderate amounts without bad effects. I would suggest that you keep their consumption to a minimum. Drink milk, water, or fruit juice in preference. Alcohol is out for the emphysema sufferer. Once in a while I drink a small glass of wine, 2 ounces or so. But for the most part, I have learned that I must avoid hard liquors, whiskeys, etc., mixed or straight.

Now, as part of this chapter, comes the subject of indigestion. First of all, try to avoid it. Now, after we have a nice case of gas (flatulence), what can we do? As I have mentioned, this is a very serious problem to the lung sufferer. If you are suffering from severe oxygen starvation, the additional strain of gas makes you suffer untold agony. Some of the most difficult and trying situations I have experienced have been due to gas pressures, which happened to occur just when my other problems were also in a critical state. There are many remedies and antacids on the market that are of some temporary assistance. However, they usually do more harm to the overall digestive process than they help. When you are suffering from a gas attack, you will find that sitting upright for a few moments, then lying back on pillows in a sitting position with your hands clasped and placed on the back of your head, will give the most relief. Try to exhale as much as possible with each breath. DO NOT PANIC! This only makes the condition worse. A few small sips of water or milk sometimes helps get the gas bubbles broken and discharged.

One of the best things I have found to stop gas distress

that is out of hand is a liquid antacid called Mylanta. It is available without prescription in all drug stores. However, do not make a *habit* of taking any antacid. Remember, use an antacid only under emergency conditions when all else fails. First, it will lose its effectiveness if you use it too often. Second, and most serious, is the interference with your natural digestive process. Americans probably use more antacids than any other medication. This use in an indiscriminate way creates a total disaster in the stomach and much harm can result from using these easily available drugs every time you turn around.

You may never be able to completely eliminate the problem of gas, but you should make every effort to learn what your system does, and how it reacts to food and drink.

One more thing that should be discussed at this time is the matter of physical activity. If you have something that must be done which will require much physical effort, such as walking a considerable distance, plan to do it on an empty stomach. You will find that this will work greatly to your advantage. It is true that the body requires food to produce energy, but the emphysema sufferer has a problem of getting enough oxygen into his blood to burn the fuel provided by the food. Thus, if you travel empty, your oxygen supply will more nearly match your available energy supply. Eating can be done after the effort is expended. I have personally practiced this for years and find it one of the useful little secrets to getting along with reduced lung capacity.

You will also want to be conscious of your bowel movements. Because of the limited room in your body, you must keep the space useful. You have no room for spent food! Fruit, fruit juice, and water in your diet will make this problem easy to solve. Remember, elimination each day is important.

Your doctor can advise you on a specific diet which will fit your particular problems. However, you must work with him and keep him informed of reactions, both good and bad.

You will want to keep a reasonably close check on your weight. A bathroom scale is a common household item or your doctor can weigh you at regular intervals.

There are many excellent books on diet and eating. I suggest that you spend a little of your time reading and learning the facts. It is a fascinating subject and can result in much benefit to the emphysema sufferer.

Summary of Chapter II

1. How the digestive system is affected by the emphysema condition.
2. How best to eat to avoid digestive stresses.
3. The importance of eating more protein and less carbohydrates.
4. The proper emotional environment during mealtime is important.
5. Programs set out as to HOW TO EAT, WHAT TO EAT, WHEN TO EAT.
6. Hints for coping with daily nutrition and health problems.

12

VITAMINS AND VITAMIN SUPPLEMENT PROGRAMS

Much has been written about the benefits of vitamins, and many amazing cures have been attributed to their use. It is the contention of most doctors that a "normal" diet supplies all the required vitamins and that vitamin programs are just "fads," without real benefit. Some of my doctors have agreed that vitamins might be beneficial and have suggested that I might supplement my diet with a good multi-vitamin preparation. Most doctors have taken a dim view of vitamin therapy, that is, the use of massive doses of vitamins to assist the body to overcome various sicknesses.

After reading several publications that dealt with vitamin therapy and the use of concentrated and massive doses in the control and cure of stress diseases and heart conditions, I decided to experiment. These experiments were the result of my own innate curiosity, guided by the best information I could gather. It seems that the condition of emphysema, in a general way, had almost escaped the vitamin experts. I will not tell you of all my trials and failures. I'll tell you only of the outstanding vitamins for use in treating emphysema. All vitamins are good and necessary to the well-being and health of the body.

We must keep in mind that there is a great difference between the so called "minimum daily requirement" of vitamins and the use of large or even massive doses of vitamins to offset malfunctions within the body.

The first vitamin I want to recommend is Vitamin C. Many protective functions are performed by this vitamin. It aids the adrenal gland to mobilize the body's defenses, stimulate the production of antibodies and white blood cells, and also increases the bacteria-destroying ability of these white blood cells.

Vitamin C is especially helpful to anyone who is suffering with the stresses of virus and bacteria infections. When your body is under heavy stress from these attacks, the blood stream becomes overloaded with toxins and poisons which must be dissipated by the already overworked lymph gland system. Massive doses of Vitamin C act to remove and neutralize, so to speak, this toxin load in your body. This is the reason why Vitamin C is often called the anti-stress vitamin by experts. I know of no one under more stress than an emphysema sufferer. Thus, Vitamin C is a natural for you.

Vitamin C is the vitamin we ordinarily associate with oranges and citrus fruit. It is often recommended as a cold fighter. Actually this vitamin is not a cold pill, and it is foolish to take it to promote an instant cure after you have neglected your body until it is sick. It is best to take a reasonable amount all the time and avoid that cold in the first place.

A victim of emphysema should use Vitamin C continually and simply vary the amount with the infection level in the lungs. Remember that this specific vitamin is the best detoxication agent available to you.

If you suffer from a very high level of infection for some period, you will probably note that your gums and the mucous membranes of your mouth bleed at night. In my case, this is a sure sign of insufficient Vitamin C. I can quickly control this bleeding condition by additional Vitaman C intake.

You will want to be especially conscious of Vitamin C when you are taking antibiotics in order to fight infections. Antibiotics have the effect of destroying Vitamin C in the bloodstream, so its replacement is of utmost importance to your health.

Vitamin C does not have a very long life in your bloodstream. Because of this fact, it should be taken often in relatively small doses. When your infection level is high, about four hours should be the maximum time between doses and two hours would be better.

I would suggest that an emphysema victim under high infection stress should take *at least* 2,000 milligrams per 24 hours. This should be divided into doses of 200 or 400 milligrams at a time. Vitamin C has never interfered with my eating or digestion, and it has never upset my stomach. Remember, massive doses are not taken all at once. I always take vitamins with milk or fruit juice.

Vitamin C, which is also called ascorbic acid, is available without prescription at drug stores, health food stores, and many food markets. I suggest you buy 100 or 200 milligram pills so as to make the dosage easier. The price of vitamins varies, so be sure to check around. All Vitamin C pills have the same chemical compound, but there is a great variety as far as combinations are concerned. Choose the one that suits you best. Just remember, Vitamin C is the cheapest toxin fighter you can buy!

Now that I have extolled the virtues of Vitamin C, I would like to discuss what I consider the most important vitamin for improvement of emphysema and that is VITAMIN E.

Emphysema victims are always suffering from lack of oxygen. In this regard Vitamin E is really incredible. VITAMIN E HAS THE EFFECT OF REDUCING THE BODY'S NEED FOR OXYGEN. Sufferers of oxygen starvation, from whatever cause, will be much improved by large concentrations of vitamin E. Vitamin E is also known to strengthen the heart muscles, which in the case of the emphysema victim is a welcome bonus, because the heart is often stressed highly during coughing spasms and breathing difficulties.

Extensive experiments have demonstrated just how effective Vitamin E can be in reducing the demand for oxygen in the body. *For example:* Healthy volunteers were divided into two groups. One group was given massive doses of Vitamin E in order to reduce the oxygen demand. The two groups were then given air with less and less oxygen content. Most of the group, which had not received the Vitamin E therapy, lost consciousness long before the group which had established a lower oxygen demand by the use of Vitamin E.

I have been using Vitamin E in various concentrations for many years. I do not feel the effect of Vitamin E as quickly or intensely as I do most medicines. After taking the vitamin for a few days, I notice that my "wind" is increased substantially and I do not become tired so easily. My level of accomplishment and my ability to do things without the usual "panting" are increased greatly. The way I can tell what this vitamin does for me is to quit taking it for a few days! My oxygen demand seems to increase greatly in just a short time. It takes quite a few days, from five to ten, to establish a new lower oxygen demand level after I start to use it again.

I take 2,000 units of Vitamin E per 24 hour day. I tried for a long time to take it in the form of wheatgerm oil, which is the primary source of Vitamin E. This oil was difficult for me to digest, and I struggled along without getting good results until I found a source of Vitamin E dispersed in a dry base.

This was at a time when my general health was much worse than at present, and I had a predetermined skepticism about the effectiveness of any vitamin, including Vitamin E. I was forcing myself, or being pressured, to take Vitamin E. Therefore, I greeted my disagreeable experience as a vindication of my opinion that it would do me no good and possibly do me harm.

Wheatgerm oil is a pleasant mild oil and very delicious when properly stored in the refrigerator and used in salad dressings, on vegetables, or any other use in which it is left uncooked. It is not necessary to gulp it down out of a spoon. It is much less expensive than the dry base preparation and since it is processed less, it is probably better for you.

Dry base Vitamin E is packaged in 200 international unit capsules. I take 1,000 units in the morning and 1,000 units at night. As usual, I take milk or fruit juice with the vitamin.

I strongly recommend the use of massive doses of Vitamin E if you want to reduce your oxygen demand. It has helped me as much as anything I have done since my trouble started 15 years ago.

Vitamins differ from medicines. Your body has a natural demand for vitamins, so there is no danger of their losing their effectiveness. Your body often builds a tolerance or accommodation to medicines so that larger and larger doses are required to be effective, and many times medicines lose their effectiveness altogether. There is no danger that your body will build an accommodation to vitamins.

Some authorities have written much about the evils of massive vitamin therapy, such as toxic side effects, etc. I do not know what long range effects all vitamins have when used in large concentrations, but I can tell you about the two vitamins I am recommending for emphysema patients. I have never recognized any harmful effects from the use of either Vitamin C or Vitamin E in the many years that I have taken large concentrations of both. Of course you will want to be guided by the advice of your doctor in all things. Your doctor may be interested to know of these results. Perhaps, none of his patients have had the opportunity to test out all of the vitamins for use in treating emphysema. Another thing to keep in mind is that your doctor isn't gasping for air. If you are, don't neglect the vitamins.

Remember again, vitamins are not medicine, and do not expect immediate results similar to medicines. The vitamins you are taking are only *adding* to the supply normally required by your body to assist it, because of abnormal circumstances, such as high infection level and oxygen starvation. Vitamins alone cannot do the job. They must become a *part* of your health program. Good food, proper rest, exercise, and proper mental attitude are among the other things which must accompany vitamin therapy for you to gain good health again.

Obtain a good book on vitamins and familiarize yourself with all of the wonderful information available today on this vital subject.

Summary of Chapter 12

1. Why vitamins are necessary for the emphysema victim.
2. Special notice taken of benefits of Vitamins C and E.
3. How to detect physical signs of need for vitamin intake.
4. How oxygen demand can be tempered with taking Vitamin E.
5. Various sources of required vitamins in foods.
6. How vitamins are an important part of the overall health program; they are not medicines.

13

EFFECTIVE MEDICATIONS

Each time we see our doctor most of us expect him to prescribe medicine to "cure" us. If we do not come away with at least one expensive prescription, we feel that our doctor is doing less than his best for us. Many people associate the doctor's office with the hypodermic injection. "My doctor gave me a shot" is a common expression. The great laboratories of the world are busily engaged in the development and testing of thousands of new drugs, and we hear of new miracle drugs and breakthroughs in the field of medicine. As with most diseases today, there are many medicines that your doctor can prescribe which may help you with your fight against emphysema. (You will note that I was careful to say *help* you and not cure you.)

In this chapter I am going to discuss some of the medicines that are available and some that doctors have used in treating me for emphysema. I here again wish to state that I am not a doctor. I am a patient. I can neither prescribe medicines nor advise you specifically regarding any one medication. No doctor could even prescribe without specific knowledge of each patient.

However, if you as an emphysema patient (and perhaps your doctor) have a knowledge of some of the various medicines available, how they work, and the specific experience of one patient with them, you can better evaluate what your doctor may be trying to accomplish in your treatment. You can, perhaps, be in a better position to work with your doctor for better and faster results. New medicines and treatments are continuously being developed and we all hope for a breakthrough in the treatment of emphysema in the near future.

Before we discuss the various medicines available, we might mention the methods used in administering medication. By this I do not mean by mouth or by injection, etc. I mean, how the dosage is given relative to time.

One method could be called continuous dosage. Once in a while a drug is considered so beneficial by your doctor that he will prescribe continuous use. Such use will consist of a dose twice a day, before each meal, or at bedtime, etc. No time limit is placed on the use of the medication. At various times my doctors have prescribed drugs to be taken in this way to treat my emphysema. I have found that medicines, regardless of type, taken at even time intervals for long periods of time tend to lose their effectiveness. I do not know what effect an increase in the size of the dosage or the frequency of the dosage might have, but without some change my body seems to develop a "tolerance" for the medicine. I choose to call this phenomenon "accommodation." In some instances the medicines have been effective for several months before accommodation was noticable. Sometimes effectiveness had been almost entirely lost in 20 or 30 days. I am sure that if the administration of the medications had been discontinued for a while, their effectiveness could have been reestablished.

You should watch for this phenomenon of accommodation in your treatments. If you observe this loss of effectiveness, discuss the possibility of a different mode of administration of medications with your doctor. I am sure that many good medications are misused because of accommodation effect, and the patient derives little, if any, good from their use. We might conclude that how a medication is administered becomes almost as important as what medication is prescribed.

Most of the medications you will receive from your doctor will be prescribed to correct a temporary condition. These prescriptions will consist of from one-day up to ten-day courses of medication to overcome an infection or other condition. After your condition is corrected, the medication is discontinued. The same medication may be prescribed at a later date if you again have the same type of attack. Medications administered in this manner seldom build up "accommodation" and their effectiveness is equally good at each treatment, unless these treatments occur too frequently.

Another method of administering medications might be termed "intermittent dosage." In this method my doctor gives me daily doses for a period of time, say one week. Then I discontinue the use of the medicine for a period of time, say three weeks. In my case of emphysema my doctor has been using intermittent administration with great success. For a long time I have found it to be most effective. I take antibiotics for ten days, each day, and then I go for 20 days without them. Then, I repeat the ten-day dosage. I follow this administration of antibiotics regardless of whether or not I have an infection or a cold. In case I do have an infectious attack or a cold, my doctor generally prescribes a more vigorous and intense usage of antibiotics, often two different kinds taken three hours apart. After the trouble has cleared up, I again discontinue the use of antibiotics for 20 days. Then I return to my regular ten-day administration and 20-day rest cycle. Using antibiotics in this fashion has helped to keep my infection level extremely low. I avoid many of the almost continuous small infections and I do not know how many major ones. I suggest you discuss this method of medicine administration with your doctor. It has been extremely successful for my emphysema.

In the following pages some of the major types of medications available for emphysema treatment will be reviewed. I am going to try to tell you what these medicines do and, approximately, how they work. Your doctor will be glad to give you more detailed and specific information on the medications he prescribes for you. I have tried to avoid using brand names, attempting instead to give you the generic or the medical name in all the cases which I can. I have made every attempt for accuracy. Since these medications are available only by doctor's prescription, your doctor will correct any of my inadvertent mistakes.

Expectorants

When infection strikes, stiff and stubborn deposits of mucus in the lung passages are an almost continual problem for the emphysema patient. Expectorants are medications which aid in expectorating or spitting by making the mucus and phlegm more fluid and easier to eject by coughing. The expectorants work two ways in your body. *First,* the mucus-producing glands are stimulated to produce more and, hence, thinner mucus to dilute the deposits. *Secondly,* the expectorant may cause additional moisture to enter into the lung tissues to perform the desired thinning. (See the discussion of positive pressure breathing apparatus in Chapter 8.)

The most effective expectorants I have used are called the iodides, especially the salt—potassium iodide. When I first used potassium iodide, my doctor prescribed orally administered pills. These pills were taken two or more times a day with good results. I now use a solution of potassium iodide. This is a saturated solution, so that it always has almost exactly the same strength all the time. The dosage is varied by the number of drops of the saturated solution. A typical dosage might be 10 to 15 drops, two to four times a day. This dosage would probably be for severe mucus conditions. If you have trouble in the mornings with stubborn deposits, you may want to use this iodide just before bedtime.

The potassium iodide solution is very bitter and quite corrosive to the sensitive mucous membranes of the mouth. Therefore, put your drops in an ounce of fruit juice. This dose should be followed by a chaser, such as water, milk, or more fruit juice. The iodides never did cause me indigestion, as such, but you may notice that your mouth has a continuous sour taste in it if you use a heavy dosage too long. This material really works. You will notice its effect within 24 hours. Once I used potassium iodide over an extensive period of time and I noted that accommodation started to set in, and it seemed to lose much of its effectiveness. However, you may never need to take the iodides for a month or more at one time. I also had a reaction to this extended use. I had a rash on my face which was similar to small boils. I have used potassium iodide subsequently on many occasions without any noticeable side effects and with complete satisfaction.

If you are allergic to the iodides or cannot tolerate them, there are other expectorants available which are just as satisfactory, but quite a bit more expensive. I used one of these products extensively and found it to perform equally as good as potassium iodide. I do not know the generic name of this product. It is a liquid with the brand name "Amilixir." Your doctor can identify the product from this name. I developed accommodation for this medicine somewhat faster than for potassium iodide. This material is very sour and should be taken with some liquid to cushion it.

All emphysema sufferers should become acquainted with the use of expectorants as they reduce the coughing effort a great deal. I was the victim of a heart seizure once, because of violent coughing. It required nine months of intensive care to allow my heart to repair itself. I was fortunate not to receive any appreciable permanent heart damage. I know from personal experience the necessity of doing everything possible to reduce the intensity and stress of coughing.

At this point, it might be well to discuss one of the newer developments in the field of medicine, which is closely allied to expectorants. Sufferers of the disease cystic fibrosis are now using a cold-fog-making machine to produce moisture in the lungs to make elimination of mucus easier. The fog-making machine nebulizes water into extremely fine particles which stay suspended in the air that is breathed by the patient for several hours a day. I have not had the opportunity to try one of these machines for my emphysema, but I do know that they are available for use in the home. Consult your doctor. Perhaps one of these units will be the answer to some of your problems.

Water

You might rightfully ask, "Can water be considered a medication?" Yes, water is probably the most important medication an emphysema patient can use. Why is it necessary for your doctor to prescribe water? Let me explain it this way. The emphysematous chest and lungs are so distended and stretched that the whole body-cavity is crowded. There just does not seem to be room enough for everything. The emphysema victim suffers when he eats a large volume of food or when he drinks a lot of fluids. In my case of emphysema, suffering is due to the fact that my lower rib cage, diaphragm, and stomach area have become so hyper-sensitive that, at times, I can actually feel liquids splashing as I walk. This is certainly a disconcerting situation and extremely difficult to tolerate. Even if you never become this sensitive, you will note how food and liquids make you have that "stuffed-up feeling." With such things as this to contend with, the emphysema victim tends to drink smaller and smaller amounts of liquids.

As you become less active, you do not perspire as heavily. Thus, you do not require as much water as you once did. However, you will find it necessary to carefully program your water intake to get sufficient moisture into your body each day. For instance, I am a mouth breather and I lose much moisture because of this fault alone. Your body is designed to give almost perfect humidity control to the air which reaches your lungs. However, the system that you are normally supposed to use to assist in adding this moisture efficiently is your nose. If you are a mouth breather, and many emphysema victims are, you will note dryness in your mouth, especially at night when sleeping. I try to off-set this with additional humidity and also by keeping drinking water at my bedside at all times. I awake several times and automatically reach for the water. I drink about two glasses each night. This helps considerably in keeping up my moisture balance. If you have difficulty in getting enough calories in your diet, you may want to substitute sweetened fruit juices for plain water during the day, whenever possible. Make an effort to develop habits which will make your water intake automatic and sufficient. Good health for the emphysema victim depends on plenty of water at all times.

Antibiotics

Your body has a most remarkable built-in defense system. When your body is attacked by bacteria and germs, a general alarm is sounded which starts action on several fronts. The infection area is often isolated by special blood vessel changes. White blood cells are made by the millions, and these blood cells attack the bacteria with great diligence. Both bacteria and white blood cells die in large numbers. At this time the body also accomplishes a most interesting and complicated medical feat. It starts to manufacture antibodies. These antibodies are remarkable substances because they are fashioned to exact specifications to destroy specific alien invaders. Your body has its own automatic medical laboratory to make prescriptions on order, so to speak. We might say that your body manufactures its own antibiotics after determining what bacteria is doing the damage. In the same way your doctor may take a sputum sample from your lungs to find out which bacteria is causing your infection in order that he can prescribe the most effective antibiotic. (See Chapter 4 dealing with infections.)

For many years medical men were able to prevent the growth of bacteria outside the body tissues with antiseptics. However, it took many years, much research, and a bit of good luck for scientists to develop medicines which would act on infective bacteria within the body without, at the same time, causing damage to the body tissues or the blood.

The age of antibiotics started in 1941 with the development of penicillin. This was the first and greatest medicine which had selective destructive action against one of man's most dangerous foes. Man had at last declared true chemical warfare against bacteria.

The requirements of an antibiotic are very exacting. It must be extremely selective in its action, killing the disease causing organism while being relatively harmless to the patient. There are dangers connected with the use of antibiotics and related drugs and they should never be used, even if available, without the specific advice of your doctor.

Bacteria are one cell organisms which multiply extremely rapidly by dividing into two. Millions of bacteria are found in the human body. Many bacteria are friendly and help with the body functions. For instance, bacteria are vital to the digestive process. Some bacteria are opportunists; they live on the skin, in the throat, lungs, and intestines. These are harmless unless they are able to penetrate living tissue after a virus invasion or other tissue destruction. Such bacteria are a constant threat to the severely damaged lung tissues of the emphysematous lung. When unfriendly bacteria attack in force, your body's defense mechanisms may lack the "punch" to defeat these invaders without outside help. Most chronic emphysema victims today will probably depend on various bacteria killing or inhibiting drugs to assist in his fight to squelch heavy infections and heal his lungs.

Do not consider antibiotics as "cure-alls." Do not use drugs as a crutch or an excuse to risk yourself, even a little bit, or expose yourself to possible infection because you have them available. Most of the antibiotics are really powerful and have a most drastic action upon the activity of the human body. Most of them have side effects of one type or another, and some people have drastic allergic reactions to certain of these drugs. When you first take any antibiotic, you should report any reactions to your doctor immediately. This may save your life or, at least, save you a lot of needless suffering.

In the hospital or clinic where you may be treated, you

will often be asked for a sputum sample. This is necessary so that the laboratory can determine what bacteria strains are causing your particular infection. Often the danger of an adverse reaction can be kept to a minimum by testing and matching the proper drug against the invading bacteria. Most of the problems associated with antibiotics would disappear if their use were confined to their known capabilities.

Most antibiotics used by emphysema victims are administered orally. These antibiotics destroy large numbers of friendly intestinal bacteria and certain vitamins, especially Vitamin C. In times of high stress you must have all your bodily functions working at high efficiency. You will need to replace the intestinal bacteria by eating yogurt twice a day or by taking a couple of tablespoons of acidophilus milk three or four times a day. You will also want to take massive doses of Vitamin C to replace that destroyed.

Penicillin

Penicillin is the modern miracle drug. Some of the most life threatening and common germs present in all sorts of invasions, such as pneumonia, scarlet fever, or infected wounds and boils, succumb to the destructive effects of penicillin. Penicillin seems to be harmless to most persons, but some have exceptional susceptibility toward it, sometimes violently so.

When I first started to fight infections, about 16 years ago, my doctors used penicillin injections with great success. Treatments generally consisted of daily injections for a period of five to seven consecutive days. This therapy was certainly effective in assisting to "cool down" the bacterial infections.

About ten years ago, I used a few treatments of what was

called "long acting" penicillin, which was supposed to keep a high level of protection in the bloodstream for 30 days or more. Before I had a chance to really test the effectiveness of the long acting protection, I developed an allergic reaction to penicillin and I cannot report on any recent effects. All I can say is that you should heed your doctor's advice on penicillin usage. If it works, use it! However, I am living proof that major lung infections can be conquered without penicillin.

You should be aware that some of the new antibiotics are very similar to penicillin. If you EVER had a reaction to penicillin of any kind, tell your doctor. This is important because you may also get a reaction to these new synthetic or penicillin-like drugs. Always carry a card or a medical alert wristband if you have known allergies. If you are in trouble and you cannot see your regular doctor, the new doctor will be aware of the problem even if you cannot talk to him.

Sulfonamides

While this drug family is not considered a true antibiotic, I am including it next because my doctors used this drug for a period of time after my adverse reaction to penicillin. Sulfonamides are usually taken orally and are absorbed into the bloodstream, thus diffusing freely to every part of the body. A high starting dose is given, followed by regular and frequent administration in order to keep up high blood levels of the drug. The use of sulfonamides is a demonstration of modern chemical and medical war strategy. Certain harmful bacteria depend on an acid called paraminobenzoic acid for growth and reproduction. This acid is found in the blood. The sulfonamides are similar to this acid and the bacteria mistakenly absorb them with disastrous results. Serious reactions and adverse side effects place limitations on the use of this drug and necessitate close supervision by your doctor.

My reaction to the use of sulfonamides is drastic loss of moisture. The tissues of my system seem to dry out at an alarming rate. The mucus in my lungs gets thick, sticky, and extremely difficult to eject. If you use this drug, discuss this moisture problem with your doctor *before* you start using it. While under treatment, drink all the water possible. If at all possible, use one of the expectorants. Do not wait to find out. By that time your lung tissues will be clogged with stiff mucus which will cause serious troubles.

I have not used sulfonamides for some time. These medications seemed to be fairly effective against my lung infections, but the moisture problem was so drastic that I now use other antibiotics which give better results.

Tetracycline

This antibiotic was developed in 1952. It is effective against a much wider range of bacteria than either penicillin or streptomycin. This series of drugs has proved to be the most effective for my emphysema and the associated infections. The drying effect of this drug is somewhat similar to the sulfonamides, although not as drastic. Moisture intake and the use of expectorants are important. Do not neglect them. Also, I should again point out the importance of replacing the intestinal bacteria by eating yogurt and also replacing the destroyed Vitamin C.

It is this family of drugs that my doctors have used so successfully with the intermittent 10-day on and 20-day off treatment described in the beginning of this chapter. I suggest you discuss such a program with your doctor.

There are many antibiotics available to the medical profession for use in the treatment of emphysema infections. To those of us who have had long debilitating illnesses, these antibiotics are certainly life savers.

Each time anyone uses one of these miracle drugs, he exposes more bacteria to the drugs. The bacteria family is then able to develop a little more resistance to the drugs. Thus, we are developing strains of germs which continuously require new and stronger drugs to control them.

Do not use antibiotics unless you really need them. Using them to control small and minor viral infections by normal people is a sin against all humanity and defeating the purpose for which medical science developed them in the first place. Take a really serious approach to your use of antibiotics and, by all means, abide by your doctor's advice in their use and administration.

Bronchial Dilators

When the lung is irritated or infected, a stimulus or a signal is developed which causes the lung passages to constrict, that is, to close down and become smaller. The lungs become more and more difficult to keep clean. Many of the small passages and entrances to the small air sacs become completely stopped-up with pieces of mucus, thus reducing materially the efficiency of the lungs. The result of course is increased shortness of breath. During periods of high infection the emphysema victim may struggle for days without letup. If we could find something which would reduce this constriction, open up those little passages, and let some air into those stagnant air sacs, we would have a wonderful helper.

Such drugs do exist. They are called bronchial dilators. To dilate means to expand or make larger. A bronchial dilator is a drug which causes the passages and tubes in the lungs to enlarge temporarily. This opening of the tubes is beneficial in two ways. *First*, it allows air to get into many of the air sacs which were completely closed off and relieves very greatly that terrible feeling of oxygen starvation. *Secondly*, much of the mucus, which is trapped, can be ejected and the lungs can be cleaned more efficiently. There are several bronchial dilators available. In cases of high duress and emergencies these bronchial dilators are a real blessing to the emphysema victim.

When we administer a bronchial dilator, we want to get the medication into the lungs, where the enlargement of the tubes is required. The drug is administered by inhaling a mist or a fog of the medication. This inhalation of mist gets the medication to the trouble area in a hurry. The medications work almost instantly, so that relief is very fast and very dynamic. Your shortness of breath (oxygen starvation) is reduced materially. The relief lasts for quite some time, allowing you to gain strength and reach a new plane of equilibrium.

Some of these dilator drugs are packaged in a small pressure can similar to the familiar paint spray or hair-set cans. These pressure capsules are about ¾ inch in diameter and 1½ inches long. These capsules are provided with a plastic mouthpiece, which is held by the hand when administering the drug The valves on the capsules are arranged to give a measured charge of mist with each squeeze. The arrangement is called a nebulizer or a "cloud maker." Some of these nebulizers do not use a pressure capsule, but use a simple atomizer to create the drug mist. In administering the drug the patient should empty his lungs quite completely before inhaling the drug, so that the dilator can get deep into the lungs where the congestion is the worst. Three, four, or five inhalations is considered a treatment. (Your doctor will direct you.)

Two types of dilators will help identify the type of dilators used by emphysema patients. One is called the Medihaler and the other, the Misto Meter. Your doctor will prescribe the particular dilator drug which he feels will do you the most good. One of these dilator drugs is called Epinephrine and another is called Isoproterenol Hydrochloride. Each type of drug is used to accomplish a specific task. So, a complete diagnosis by your doctor will dictate the one which is for you. See Figure 13-1 for using a nebulizer.

Figure 13-1. Using the nebulizer in order to inhale bronchial-dilator mist.

Bronchial dilators are also available in orally administered pills. The pills are not so dramatic in their effect, but perhaps your doctor will advise these for you instead of the nebulizer type.

Dilators should be used for times of duress when you are suffering severe shortness of breath and oxygen starvation due to infection and heavy mucus deposits. Dilators will not restore your "wind" if you have been walking or exercising and are "puffing" for air due to these efforts. The bronchial dilator is so very dramatic in its relief that you are liable to let it become a crutch, using it when you do not really need it or, worse, when it cannot possibly help you. I have observed quite a few lungers who carry one of the nebulizers around all the time and use the drug indiscriminately when they feel breathless, regardless of cause. THIS MEDICATION IS NEITHER OXYGEN NOR IS IT A SUBSTITUTE FOR OXYGEN. If you walk or exercise, you will become breathless and "short of wind." The bronchial dilator cannot restore your equilibrium. Oxygen supply and carbon dioxide elimination are the only things that can do this in most instances.

After using bronchial dilators for a considerable length of time, I became concerned about the possibility that this medication might cause a permanent enlargement of the lungs. This, of course, would be bad because the emphysematous lung is already too large. I discussed this with my doctors and they assured me that the dilation was temporary in nature and that no permanent enlargement would result. Nevertheless, this thought made me realize that this is indeed a potent drug and that I should use it for emergencies only. I have not used these drugs much in the last five years, but my doctor advises me to keep them available for use if I require them.

I found that the dilators had little, if any, side effects. Once in a while, when I inhale them, I feel "cottony" or have a sensation similar to that imparted by the inhalation of lacquer thinner vapors. This sensation is not very comforting, but it is relatively short-lived.

Influenza Inoculation

The deep lung infections, which are almost always the result of serious epidemics of Asian flu sweeping the nation every year, make it mandatory for the lunger to do everything possible to protect himself. You should have your flu inoculation every fall, that is, if your doctor agrees. The cost is certainly small and your reaction to the inoculation will be negligible when it is compared to the flu itself. I was very apprehensive about these inoculations for many years. I was always afraid I would suffer terrible reactions that would be as bad as the disease. So for years I avoided them. Then, one year a bout with Asian flu put me in the hospital for ten days. It took me about five months to overcome the ravages of that attack. This convinced me that I must have those inoculations at all costs. The first year my doctor divided the customary inoculations into two parts, giving half doses at two week intervals. I had very little reaction. Thus, this experience proved that I was simply wrong about adverse reaction to flu inoculations. I strongly recommend that you discuss this preventive medication with your doctor immediately. If you can avoid influenza or, at least, reduce the intensity of an attack, you will have won a major victory.

Cough Medicines

So-called cough medicines include a wide classification of drugs. You can go to your drugstore and purchase numerous preparations in the form of liquids, pills, and lozenges (mostly medicated candy).

Coughing is synonymous with lung trouble of some magnitude. Coughing is caused by irritation or by foreign materials and mucus in the lungs. The purpose of the cough is to forcibly eject matter from the lungs. Coughing is a necessary function of life. However, when the lungs are hypersensitive, due to infection, virus, smoking, or dust, the cough may continue when there is no material to eject. This is termed the "nonproductive cough." This type of cough is your enemy. Sleep is lost and you suffer much agony. Your doctor should by all means prescribe a good cough medication to deaden that "tickle" in your throat, so that you can get proper sleep and rest. The real object of the game is to get rid of the irritation that is causing the cough. If your cough is from smoking, *stop*. If your cough is from smog or dust, move or get an efficient filter for your home. In order to heal those lungs you must master the irritation problem. A cough medicine, at its best, is only a temporary expedient as far as a nonproductive cough is concerned. Find out why you have that "hack." Then, correct the cause! Do not "lean" on cough medicine for this!

There is no way, however, for an emphysema victim to eliminate coughing entirely. The cough you will use will be the productive cough which assists in cleaning your lungs. The productive cough will produce mucus and phlegm. When virus attacks penetrate deeply into your lung tissues, you may suffer from a nonproductive cough condition. Then, a cough medication will assist to gain rest and sleep. Often cough medications for an emphysema victim are combined with an expectorant, so that the resulting preparation accomplishes two necessary duties.

Cough medications have often helped me through bad infections. I find them especially useful on retiring to make it easier to get to sleep when virus infections are creating much irritation.

In recent years my lung condition has improved so that I have less and less infections. I cough a small amount each morning, but aside from that, I have virtually eliminated my need to cough. I do not use cough medicines much these days.

Cortisone and ACTH

The adrenal gland produces several hormones which operate to keep the body's defense mechanism against infections operating in perfect balance. These various hormones control the production of white blood cells and antibodies which are the bacteria and virus killers. Some other of these hormones work to control what doctors call an inflammatory reaction in the area of the infection or irritation.

One of the important hormones secreted by the adrenal gland at times of infection stress is called cortisone. The hormone cortisone is sometimes called the stress hormone. Cortisone in the correct amounts is closely associated with the control of inflammation in the body. When the body is under long stress due to a serious infection, the adrenal gland gets tired, so to speak, and does not produce enough cortisone.

This drug, cortisone, is mostly associated with the treatment of arthritis. However, my doctors have prescribed short series of orally administered cortisone pills when my infection level was very high and I was under great stress. The use of cortisone certainly "cools off" the inflammation sensations for me. I consider this drug only a temporary expedient and I do not believe it is an effective treatment as far as improvement of emphysema conditions is concerned.

Scientists have also discovered that another hormone produced by the pituitary gland controls the production of cortisone by the adrenal gland. This hormone is known by the medical abbreviation ACTH. Sometimes doctors use ACTH injections instead of giving cortisone. The extra ACTH then stimulates the adrenal gland to produce the needed cortisone. I have used ACTH injections with essentially the same results as taking cortisone pills.

When I was using cortisone and ACTH, my doctors were always very concerned about side effects, toxin level in my blood, and other things. They were always careful to limit the dosage to a few days at a time.

Tranquilizers

Doctors have not often prescribed tranquilizers for my use. The few times that I have used these drugs, I have had very unsatisfactory results. Tranquilizers seem to have the effect of depressing my breathing ability. The feeling of oxygen starvation is increased materially by the use of these drugs. My general reaction could be described as one of nervous fatigue. I suggest that if your doctor prescribes these drugs, you should use extreme caution until you are completely acquainted with all of their effects on you.

Body Temperature

When the normal body is sick or infected, the body temperature rises several degrees above normal. The sick person is said to have a fever. When a doctor is first examining you, one of his first measuring sticks to determine the seriousness of your illness is his thermometer. If the thermometer shows a high fever, you are considered to be very ill and worthy of emergency treatment.

Low-grade infections in the area of the windpipe do not necessarily cause a rise in body temperature. The lungs can produce mucus and phlegm without any temperature rise.

Some unlucky people, like myself, never run much of a temperature regardless of their condition. The body temperature controls are very complex and some of us are "freaks," so to speak, when it comes to fever. If you are one of these unfortunate people, be forewarned. The thermometer is not necessarily the true measure of your infection. Most doctors probably recognize this today, but if you find yourself in this category do not be afraid to mention it to any doctor who does not know you. Infections must be fought when they start, regardless of thermometer readings, body temperature or anything else. A day lost at the beginning of a serious infection attack can mean an extra week or even a month spent in undeserved suffering.

Your Approach to Medicines

Remember medicines are prescribed to assist your body to help itself. Do not expect your medications to help you unless you help them with proper diet, rest, attitude, and clean living habits. In America we have come to expect too much of medicines without giving of our time and effort to the cure of our ailments. We are interested in miracles, not assistance.

Summary of Chapter 13

1. Author's experience with various medicines prescribed by his doctors; possible benefits for others in working with their doctors.
2. Continued use of a medicine often reduces its effectiveness.
3. The function of expectorants; use of potassium iodide.
4. Drinking adequate water is essential.
5. The benefits and side effects of antibiotic therapy are discussed and evaluated.
6. Use of bronchial dilators, tranquilizers, influenza immunizations, cortisone and miscellaneous medicines discussed; thermometer not necessarily a true indicator of existing infection.

14

HOW TO COPE
WITH FEAR

Man has an inherent fear of drowning. Anyone who has had much experience swimming or playing in the water, has probably experienced a few moments of panic or near-panic when it seemed that he was going to lose his air supply. Fear is always associated with oxygen starvation. Those who have not personally experienced the horrors and fears of oxygen starvation cannot completely understand or sympathize.

The chronic emphysema patient is often like a drowning man. In fact you may almost "drown" many times a day. Violent coughing spasms leave one gasping and fighting for just enough air to exist. After such coughing spasms, you struggle with your breathing a long time before you are able to regain your oxygen balance. During severe infection attacks, the discharge from the lungs becomes so great and so sticky, that at times it actually feels as if your entire air supply will be shut off and that you will really choke to death. Fright is always the result of such attacks.

After you have had numerous infections and have learned how your body reacts, you will notice that your heart and nervous system anticipate a choking spasm some time before you can actually feel the constriction in your throat. Your heart will start to beat with great rapidity and your nervous system will react in such a way that you can antic-

ipate the coming emergency. This forewarning sensation
is not a pleasant one and fear is immediately associated
with the forewarning.

One thing about suffering from lung infection is that
there is little, if any, actual "pain" as such. I do not say
there is no agony and no suffering. Far from it. But there
is no pain. Perhaps we could say that fear is a substitute
for pain in the case of oxygen starvation.

During periods of intense duress, while attempting to
cough up the phlegm and pus, *fear* always takes over. It
makes no difference how many times you go through these
emergencies and finally are able to raise the material, discharging it from your lungs. Each time, you again panic.
Fear becomes your master.

Now, I know that it is easy to give advice on such subjects, but in my own case, I still suffer from fear even after
many years of observing it in myself. Regardless of all this,
the old rule, DON'T PANIC, still applies.

The extra strain placed on your system by fear only makes
things worse, so try to reflect on past emergencies you have
had and how you were able to overcome them. When you
are under emergency conditions, one of the greatest helps
is to have someone with you. There is little, if anything,
anyone can do to really assist you. However, another person's presence does relieve the tension a great deal.

Once when I was in a hospital, my room was near the
service desk. When I would have a violent coughing fit,
nurses (yes, more than one) would rush to my bed and
then simply stand there, helplessly watching me fight.
There wasn't anything they could do, but I sure did appreciate their presence.

When I am under the worst conditions of choking and
coughing, I always want the windows and doors open.
This helps to relieve the tension. Sit or stand in the position

which gives you the most relief. Do not worry about getting chilled or too cold as you can get warm after the emergency is over. To tell the truth, the exertion of coughing will keep you very warm. This admonition is for the helpful soul who is determined to wrap you up in a cocoon to keep you out of a draft. You will need those blankets when the emergency is over and your energy and body heat are spent, not in the middle of the spell, when the pressure on your shoulders is unbearable.

Use your oxygen supply if you have one. I find that a tube blowing oxygen into my face, so that some enters my mouth and nose, is a way to relieve tension. Whether the oxygen does any good, as such, is not the important thing.

Sometimes a very, I repeat, a very gentle massage of the back, along the backbone and ribs, will help to relieve tension and aid the regaining of your equilibrium.

You will never get over fighting your enemy, fear. I have discussed this with my doctors at various times and they assure me that their records show that no one has choked to death with phlegm or mucus in the windpipe or upper lung tubes in such a condition as my emphysema. This knowledge gives me great comfort until I am under great duress. Then, the old enemy, fear, takes over and it again takes high resolve and almost superhuman effort to endure the agonies of the coughing spasm.

Often fear is created by anticipation: If you face a particular situation, which you feel might place you under strain or duress, fear enters the picture and you are not at your best to meet any emergency which might occur. An emphysema victim develops a special fear of the unknown. For instance, in traveling you are always so concerned with the walking distance required at the airport and whether you have to climb stairs to get there, etc., that you actually miss much of the joy associated with the various activities of traveling. When going to a meeting, most people are thinking about what they will say and do after they arrive. The emphysema patient has only one concern and that is, getting to the meeting! Often he loses most of his value and effectiveness because of fear.

This constant dread of new situations is common to all emphysema victims. You are always afraid you will get into a situation where you just can't make it! The main thing I have found to help me with this fear is to have a companion, if possible, at all times. The other thing which has helped is to keep teaching myself that I do not have to establish a speed record. Let the world wait!

I am sorry that I do not have a formula for you to use to completely conquer this problem of fear. But, perhaps just sharing with you the fact that the problem exists with all chronic emphysema patients will assist you to a better understanding and lessening of your problem.

One other thing which might be well to mention is that problem of claustrophobia. Claustrophobia is the doctor's name for a fear of being closed in or being confined in a small space. As your lung condition becomes more severe, you will naturally develop a special type of fear of smothering or being caught in a place where there is a small and insufficient air supply. This fear extends somewhat, until at times, I have been afraid to sit in a car with all of the windows up. A small, closed room seems like a prison until a window or door is opened.

This fear, claustrophobia, is a natural one and you should learn to live with it. Explain this weakness to your family, friends, and associates. They will no doubt respect your problem and assist you. When and if you are caught in a situation where this fright of being closed in starts to get the better of you, try to resolve it by remembering that unless the space in which you are temporarily confined is extremely tight you will get enough air to sustain your life for many hours. If you panic, you will dissipate energy and use up available air sooner!

Another situation from which the lunger suffers much agony is crowds or crowded rooms. This could be a form of claustrophobia. But, in the case of the crowded room the oxygen content of the air is reduced somewhat and, of course, the carbon dioxide level is raised so that the sensitive lunger notices the difference. This intensifies his oxygen starvation sensations.

I talked to one lung patient who even had a fear of darkness when he was under severe oxygen starvation. His wife, who did not know of this fear, was naturally horrified to realize that she had added to his discomfort in any way, just by turning out the light so he could sleep. He had felt that it was silly and never mentioned it to her.

Whatever your fear may be, do not be sensitive about it. Tell your family, doctor, and nurses of your problem. They will be more than glad to cooperate with your weakness. Anything which will help you, regardless of how silly you may think it appears, should be done. There is no harm in any of these small things and if you are relieved from fear in any way, you are a step closer to your ultimate goal of recovery.

I feel that a thorough understanding of emphysema, how the lungs work, and how the medical profession has worked out various methods of treatment will help the patient to overcome fear to some degree. At least you will have a better grasp of many situations which used to be strange. This should reduce your tendency to panic.

Recent studies have indicated that people who weather a crisis well are those who actively search for a solution. They thirst for helpful information. They want to know in advance exactly what to expect in any given situation. They avoid blaming themselves or others, realizing that this is a distraction from the real problem. They are not afraid to express fears and anxieties. They learn how to rest when their efficiency falls because of fatigue, and how to discipline themselves to return to the painful struggle when they have been replenished. They can accept, even enlist, help, considering this not a sign of weakness, but of maturity. Try to apply these simple principles to your problems of fear associated with the condition of emphysema.

Summary of Chapter 14

1. Fear as a destructive factor in an emphysema victim's life.
2. Sensations of fear and oxygen starvation—how they are associated.
3. Dread of new or strange situations; how to handle.
4. How a basic understanding of body functions can help calm fears.
5. Claustrophobia, tendency to panic, and other mental causations of fear; how to handle them
6. The use of bottled oxygen to relieve fears.
7. When under "duress," remember your breathing exercises.

15

THE IMPORTANCE OF
MENTAL ATTITUDE

Of all the things there are to discuss regarding emphysema, I believe that your attitude, your philosophy, is the most important. The everyday grind, continuous reversals, colds, flu, bad weather, or the fight just to exist place great pressure on the emphysema sufferer. The small things in life, such as going to the kitchen to get a drink of water, become large and almost insurmountable problems. Tasks like shaving, washing your face, and combing your hair become real projects. So many small things, which you used to do without even noticing you were performing them, are now beyond your reach.

This inability to "do" is extremely frustrating to a person who was once active. Your natural reaction is one of irritation and you can inflict a great deal of stress upon yourself. Also, you may strike out at those about you in your effort to find an outlet for your desires to move and do things that normal people around you are doing all the time. You must learn all over again to live at a different rate of speed, just like a racing car driver getting used to the crawl of the morning freeway.

This learning and adjusting will not be easy. In fact, it is the hardest thing an emphysema sufferer has to do. Your irritations will at times turn to a form of self-pity. You will feel so so sorry for yourself! This self-pity is a disease, even worse than emphysema, and the result may be to simply give up.

IF YOU EVER GIVE UP AND JUST GO TO BED AND STAY THERE FOR ANY LENGTH OF TIME, THE CHANCES ARE GOOD THAT YOU WILL NEVER WALK AGAIN.

Now, to overcome this greatest of all dangers, that is, giving up, develop two lines of attitude. *First,* develop the power of right thinking. You must realize and believe that *you can* improve your condition. This improvement will be painfully slow, but if you follow the general treatments I have outlined in this book, you can and will improve. The first requirement is to really believe you can improve. This gives you the heart and the drive to fight and to try, again and again, against almost insurmountable odds.

The second quality you must cultivate is patience. It has been said, "Patience is the only virtue." I certainly know of nothing which will test one's patience like emphysema. There just isn't any complete relief during the waking hours of your life. Before attempting the smallest task, you must calculate the cost in energy. Can I get there? Can I do it? Will I be forced beyond my endurance? Will I cause embarrassment to myself? Others?

This situation makes it necessary for you to remember that parts of your body are working *harder* to make up for the shortage caused by oxygen starvation. Your straining in an emotional sense to overcome obstacles will only add to the stress that your body is already under.

Now the kind of patience I am talking about here is not "submissive patience" which we ordinarily might associate with the trials and tribulations of life over which we have no control. The kind of patience I speak of might be called "practical patience" or "intelligent patience." By this I mean that you can be assured that a carefully planned course of action will give you improvement. A practical approach will be one of waiting with a purpose. However, you must be prepared for a long struggle. Your progress will be so painfully slow that you will require almost superhuman qualities to keep your spirits up. You must keep up your interest in things going on about you. Do not become a recluse or hermit. Read a daily paper or have someone read it to you. Read current magazines, listen to news programs, keep up your interest in sports, see if you can develop a hobby, or learn a foreign language! Do something!

Your wife or husband can be of great assistance to you in keeping the proper mental approach to your problem. Remember, your attitude is as important to your improvement as all the doctors and medicines in the world.

Do not become self-centered. Devote time to helping others, have an interest in things which will help others. Learn to be a good listener. Do not complain to·others continuously of your sufferings. Always have a positive outlook on your condition. Talk over your problems with your doctor. Tell him of your fears or the things you feel he can "explain away." Your doctor can give you a more positive grip on your life.

Because improvement is so painfully slow at times, I found that setting small goals of accomplishment of physical things often gave me a much needed mental boost. For instance, I described how to count steps when taking walking exercises in your home. I used to set goals of "another trip around next time" or "30 more steps tomorrow." These small things seem quite silly to a normal person, but to a lunger they become very real. Self-assurance and self-confidence are gained by simply knowing that your abilities are really improving.

One of the best ways to improve your mental attitude toward your problem is to reach a better understanding of your body, how and why it works, and how emphysema affects the function of your body. Study the material in this book and other articles in current magazines. Study the reaction your body has to the various suggested treatments. This understanding will give you positive thinking. You will learn to recognize the symptoms, be prepared to cope with emergencies, and know what to expect in almost all phases of your illness.

I believe that my own *active* interest in my emphysema condition is one reason why I have been able to make such strides in improvement. Of course everyone is interested in their own condition and how they feel. This is "passive" interest and not what you should have at all! What I am referring to here is *active interest*. Make improving a business. Run your business to make a profit. Keep your business going 24 hours per day. Your profit will be improved health; something money cannot buy!

Above all, you are going to have to be strict with yourself. You are going to be required to develop a high degree of regimentation of your daily conduct to develop self-discipline. If you do not do this, it is easy for an emphysema victim to become a vegetable. You must take care of your personal requirements each day, if at all possible. Keep your appearance neat. Shave, watch the condition of your skin, nails, etc. This will require effort on your part, but if you allow yourself to become dissipated, it is just that much harder to come back.

TRY, this is the secret. The simple word "try." You have many years of strain and stress ahead, but you only have to live them one day at a time. So, develop the proper attitude. It will make your other problems simpler to solve.

The secret to healthy adaptation is your ability to face up to the situation, despite its stress and unpleasantness, and despite the inevitable setbacks which you will no doubt suffer.

Summary of Chapter 15

1. Why good mental attitude contributes so importantly to the emphysema victim's well-being.

2. How to develop the knack of "intelligent patience."

3. The importance of a positive outlook on life and what it can do for the emphysema victim.

4. The benefits of setting goals of physical accomplishment; basic programs.

5. How getting more knowledge about emphysema and methods of controlling it helps develop a right attitude.

6. The necessity of keeping up self-esteem and denying self-pity.

16

HOW TO
LIVE WITH THE
EMPHYSEMA PATIENT

This subject is covered to help not only the patient, but most particularly, the one who is going to live with the patient, whether it is husband, wife, child, or nurse.

One thing you must understand is that emphysema is not a temporary disease; it is a condition. Although improvement can be made in the condition, the basic problem is lifetime in extent. Therefore, you may as well learn to adjust your household and your living methods in order to match this condition. Many people will assume that they can get "cured," as with other diseases, and will simply refuse to recognize that bronchial insufficiency is a fact of their life. The result is continual frustration.

To begin with, the emphysema patient will require a lot of extra apparatus around the house to make his treatment possible. Do not try to hide this equipment, but make it comfortable and easy to use, easy to clean, and easy to get at. Such things as a slope board for postural drainage, oxygen bottles, positive pressure breathing apparatus, and a hospital bed are things which will be in the home occupied by the lung patient.

Medications will, at times, become numerous and very

careful and systematic care of these will keep order, prevent accidents, and save money. Prescriptions for many of the medications are very expensive and every effort should be made to get them filled as economically as possible. Be sure that your doctor's prescriptions indicate that they can be refilled, if such is the case, so that you can obtain refills without the inconvenience of having to find your doctor every time you run low on a vital antibiotic, expectorant, or other medication. Somehow you always run out on Sunday afternoon.

Always have your doctor give the generic name of the drugs you use, so that your druggist will be able to fill your prescription with the least expensive preparation at his disposal. (Get the name of the drug, not the brand name.) Sometimes there is a startling difference in the price of the same preparation under two different names. I have found that all drugstores do not charge the same for prescriptions. A little research will save you much money in the terms of a year. For example, there are associations of retired persons whose sole function is to provide prescriptions, vitamins, and medical supplies for people on a fixed income. If you qualify, it would be well worth the time to locate them. The initial fee is under $5, and the savings are considerable. Also, it is possible that you might purchase this type of merchandise through your union. Make a business of getting the best provisions for your emphysema patient, but at the most reasonable price.

Keep all of your receipts, as you know that medical expenses are tax deductible. However, you must prove your deductions. It would be difficult to expect a tax examiner to believe the amount that you will spend each year in keeping this condition in check without proof.

The main thing in living with the emphysema patient is

order and a systematic approach. There are so many things to do in order to just exist. The patient seems to have time for nothing else but treatments. You should strive to arrange things in your household so that these necessary activities are as nearly automatic as you can make them. Establish a routine and stick by it. This will give you much more time for other pursuits.

The wife or husband must learn to cope with the patient's problems. He or she must learn many of the things discussed in Chapter 15 dealing with attitudes. Patience, perseverance, and positive approach are among those attributes which must be developed.

The helper will many times have to insist that a routine prescribed by your doctor be followed. Be sure that medications are given as prescribed. If medications are not taken at regular intervals, their effectiveness is lost. Make this a must during periods of high infection level.

Go to the doctor with your husband or wife who has emphysema. Listen carefully to the instructions that your doctor gives. Follow instructions!

Heat, cooling, air, ventilation, cleanliness, and orderliness will be things which he will expect to become automatically taken care of. The paramount thing is to make life as easy and pleasant for the patient as is possible. A little extra work to provide permanent facilities in the home for the emphysema patient will give stability and confidence to your patient.

Since the number one result of emphysema is frustration, some attempt should be made to replace traveling and other strenuous activities, which were formely a routine thing, with less strenuous interests which, nevertheless, are stimulating and mutually up-building. Real happiness or contentment is seldom found at 90 miles an hour. If your life's companion cannot walk with ease, it will not draw you together if you suddenly decide to devote all of your spare time to tennis.

The improvement of your patient must always be your first order of business. However, remember that, in case of your husband for example, you are not dealing with a petulant child and you are not a jailor. A reasonable person with emphysema will not attempt things which are really beyond his capacity. Under no circumstances should you overprotect and, consequently, turn him into a vegetable. He does not have the strength to fight both you and his condition. Let him use his limited strength to improve his endurance. The body that is not used to capacity, regardless of what that capacity is, loses its ability to be used at all.

Driving an automobile is an example of an activity that can be carried on by a person with emphysema, but must be accomplished when he is feeling at his best and not under duress; for example, no rushing to the airport at 8 o'clock in the morning, in heavy traffic. The same person is well able to negotiate most any trip of reasonable length later in the day. Of course, power steering and brakes are desirable for the reduction of fatigue.

You probably are not a trained nurse, but trained or not, there are some things which you will have to master. Learn to give a decent bed bath. Take care of his clothing and skin to prevent bedsores when he is confined to bed for a few days or weeks. Remember that your number one project is to protect your patient from colds and bronchial infections to the extent of your power to do so. An important phase of this program is to educate other members of the family. (See the discussion of infection in Chapter 4.)

As a good housewife, you will be concerned about the

clean and fresh appearance of the surroundings of your patient. But, when you clean, *don't make dust!* Use the vacuum cleaner, damp cloths, and don't ever sweep where your patient is. Remember, every thing that you stir up into the air is going to go into the air that your lunger has to breathe.

It takes a paragon of tact and resourcefulness to make sure that the victim of emphysema, who feels terrible in the morning at best and feels better as the day progresses, does not stay up too late at night. That is when he feels best and he hates to turn it off. Don't threaten him with the morning. He does need rest and sleep. His exertion is so great that he needs more than most people. It is up to you to see that he gets it.

In this day and age when everyone from the age of 12 smokes, it is sometimes difficult to protect your patient from smoke in the air around him. This is a place that calls for firm measures, if tact doesn't work. All the garbage that is exhaled in your air is going to be breathed by the one who is having troubles on good air.

I think that we should also say something about the self-sacrificing spouse who allows himself or herself to become rundown, wan, and tired, while bravely carrying on. This is a ridiculous and possibly fatal mistake. Not fatal for themselves, but rather for the trusting soul who is expecting them to be on hand when needed. Care for and nurse the emphysema victim, but by all means protect yourself from infection! A cold for you probably means that your patient is going to stand a terrible hazard of getting it too.

The emphysema patient should realize that his nurse (wife, child, etc.) deserves some amount of normal activity and association. Because emphysema requires almost constant 24 hour a day attention, your companion often loses touch with the world, so to speak. Each household should make some definite arrangement to give the nurse an opportunity for rest and relaxation away from her duties in the sickroom at regular intervals.

Above all things, have a sense of humor and a cheerful attitude. Remember that emphysema is a grim thing and you do not need to add to the gloom with words or attitude. Be aware of the improvement of your patient and encourage him to develop discipline and to work at his improvement continually. You can have a great deal to do with his desire to live as well as his ability to do so.

Summary of Chapter 16

1. The necessity of being reconciled to the fact that emphysema is a life-long condition.

2. How to make apparatus at home accessible and simple to use for any situation.

3. Medical records to be maintained.

4. How to compensate for loss of previous physical activities; possible substitutes suggested.

5. The best environment to maintain for both the emphysema victim and the one taking care of him.

6. Important hints on maintaining favorable morale.

17

TIPS ON GETTING UP IN THE MORNING

As we have indicated several times in this book, the morning is the time of misery and trouble for the emphysema sufferer. Healthy people who awake, arise, and start the day with a song cannot even imagine taking two to three hours everyday just to get up! Talk about the lost weekend! The lunger probably loses at least three hours per day, on the average, just getting the old body started, so to speak. Consequently, most victims of emphysema really live a 21 hour day, more or less. The process of getting started requires so much energy and concentration that nothing else can be expected of the awakening patient. I have often thought that this time would be useful to learn a foreign language, read a good book, etc., but it is not! Your total concentration is required to carry on the necessary bodily functions.

This chapter is devoted to comments and suggestions for your consideration and use without much evaluation. In this discussion I am going to be quite intimate about coughing and eliminating mucus from the lungs. This picture I am painting is not a pretty one, but then again, this book is written for sick people. I want to tell you about your problem in a frank, down-to-earth way, so as to help you as much as I can. I believe that sharing these things will greatly assist those who are really suffering from emphysema and those who are caring for them. If you cannot share in this information, then you are not sick or do not know someone who is. So, you do not need to read it anyway. Emphysema is neither pretty nor nice, so discussing the problems encountered is not always so nice either.

Checkpoints on Getting Up in the Morning and Special Notes Regarding Coughing.

The following tips have proved invaluable to me and may be of some assistance to you, the emphysema victim.

1. Your primary objective will be to free the lungs of the overnight accumulation of mucus and phlegm.

2. If you must be ready to "go" at 8:00 A.M., start your getting up at 5:30. This may seem silly to those who do not know the problem, but time is the most important factor in easing the pains of starting your day.

3. Empty your bladder as soon as possible to give your lungs all the room they can get.

4. The first thing to do is to use your slope board for 20 minutes or so if you have sufficient discharge to warrant it.

5. In any event, you will want to get your torso vertical at an early time to start the elimination process.

6. If you use a positive pressure breather, now is the time. The moisture from this unit will sometimes help greatly in loosening the night's deposits.

7. Have many pillows on your bed so that you can rest in a sitting position.

8. Hot coffee or tea seems to assist in loosening the deposits of mucus, which have dried in the upper trachea. Do not drink much of it; just breathe the vapor from it. If you do not have a positive pressure breathing machine, you will find that inhaling steam, through your mouth from a cup of something hot will be very helpful.

9. Have water at your bedside at all times.

10. Do not force yourself. If you cannot get going in time, so what? Better to be late than to have a heart seizure because of over-exertion.

11. Try to do everything to control your coughing. If you cannot loosen the deposit, stop coughing, which is a hard thing to do, and wait awhile.

12. I have found that talking is very effective in jarring loose especially sticky mucus in my windpipe.

13. Do not take food, pills, or vitamins, until you have expelled the worst of the mucus. Your body is in enough trouble without trying to force things down while you force things up.

14. Try "deep breathing" during rest periods to restore your strength and oxygen balance.

15. Have plenty of tissues at hand.

16. Don't panic.

17. You will become very nauseous at times; gagging will be a common thing. Do not let this alarm you. The gagging somewhat assists in loosening the material in your upper windpipe.

18. After the rigors of the elimination are over, allow yourself at least 20 to 30 minutes of rest to gain your complete equilibrium.

19. If at all possible, have someone with you during very bad mornings. This relieves the tension considerably.

20. After your elimination and rest, you can take your first nourishment, such as milk with food concentrates.

21. Be extremely careful not to choke when taking liquids. This is disastrous in the morning.

22. Use your oxygen if you feel it will assist you. This is the time to take all of the strain that you can off your heart and body.

23. During periods of high duress, if someone can read to you or divert your attention, you can generally get through better.

24. Your wife or husband should be your valet. Your clothes, shoes, etc., should be selected and made available to you without any great effort or confusion.

25. Have someone do such things as tie your shoes or put on your shoes and stockings. Strangely enough, this task, which requires you to double over and compress your lungs, will put more stress on your body than severe exercise will to a normal person.

26. After you rest, you should assume a standing position and keep standing for quite a while because this change of position to a full standing one is quite a strain on the emphysema victim.

27. If you can have a "bar" or table of the correct height so that your elbows rest comfortably on it, you can gain your standing equilibrium in two stages. It is done, first, by "leaning" for a while and, then, actually standing.

28. Always remember that your hands behind your head is a good position to promote chest flexibility. It will also assist in times of heavy breathing duress.

29. It goes without saying that during this awakening period, you will want fresh air in your room.

30. Because you go through this same routine every day, you should have all your "gear" in proper order, so that all the aids you will require will be immediately available at all times.

31. This is the time when that old enemy, *fear*, creeps in! Remember that you were able to get through yesterday's emergency, so no doubt you can get through today too.

32. If you are having an especially tough time, have your wife or nurse rub your back very lightly. This will reduce tension.

33. Keep the inside of your mouth wet at all times. This will assist in getting some moisture down into those dried out lungs.

34. The longer you wait before starting to cough, the easier it will be to eliminate the deposit. Waiting, generally, allows some mucus and moisture from above and below to "soak" and dilute the stiff deposit in your windpipe.

35. By concentration you can learn to tolerate the mucus

in your windpipe while you establish your equilibrium by deep breathing.

36. Try clearing your throat with a motion that "rattles" the upper windpipe. This rattling will often greatly assist in breaking loose that stubborn deposit.

37. The feeling of mucus rattling and moving in the windpipe is one of the most exasperating things in the world. You must learn how to tolerate this. You must learn how to cough! Do not feel compelled to expel all of the mucus. Remember, coughing is your worst enemy. It simply tears your lungs apart. If you will learn how to cough in stages, that is, raise a little mucus and then allow it to remain in your upper windpipe and then raise a little more etc., you will find that coughing is a lot less violent and that the larger deposits are easier to get up and spit out. For example: I know that at one time or another you had guests or were at a meeting and, because of the situation, you were forced to control your cough. You had mucus in your upper windpipe which caused you to cough in small bursts, but you were able to control it for a long time before being free to eject the mucus deposit. Remember how easy the material came out? This is really the way we should try to do our coughing. Keep from trying to eject every little piece of material. This often causes the violent bursts which are the ones that tear up your lungs.

38. Keep in mind that your lungs are always productive to some degree and, at most any stage of emphysema or infection, you are not going to get rid of all the material. There will no doubt be some more

mucus produced later. Therefore, look on your coughing and spitting as a continuous cleaning process. If you learn this, you will not cough like every piece of mucus is the last. It seems strange that a man should be required to take "coughing lessons," but that is about the size of it.

39. Remember that a great deal of extra stress is placed on your heart by all this morning exertion. Do everything you can to reduce your work load so that your heart will not be pushed to the limit unnecessarily.

40. Your relationship with the outside world will be affected greatly by your morning condition. Even though you may be able to get your body going at a reasonable hour, you will no doubt be suffering from the adverse conditions shared by all emphysema victims in the morning. In order to be fair to yourself and others, you should make every attempt to schedule any meetings or conferences in the afternoon or early evening hours. Your employer should be advised of this situation so that he can make some adjustments and, thereby, make use of your services when you are at your best. I have found that almost everyone is more than willing to cooperate when the situation is explained.

41. The "morning miseries" will be the acid test regarding your attitude. (See Chapter 15.) This is when "practical patience" must be practiced with diligence. When you are confronted with conditions of duress and oxygen starvation is causing you so much agony, it is often very difficult to be civil to anyone. You just seem to strike out at the very hand that is trying to assist you. Your nurse or assistant

should recognize this tendency and learn to make allowances for your problem. However, you should not use your condition as an excuse to be intolerable every morning. Keep struggling with your emotions until they are stabilized and you are able to control yourself effectively.

42. Because you will daily go through the "morning phase," you should give extremely careful consideration to every possible point which will assist you.

Evaluate the material presented in this book. The subject matter has been divided in such a way that you can consider your problem from many aspects. Go over the morning program with your nurse and other members of your household. Perhaps they will have helpful suggestions. Consult your doctor as to the correctness of any therapy which you may improvise. Read each chapter in a searching manner to see if you can find one or more things which will reduce your distress in some way.

Summary of Chapter 17

There are 42 specific tips or guidelines set out in this chapter for the emphysema victim to follow upon arising and getting set for the day. This period is a critical one in the emphysema victim's day-to-day living, and requires total concentration to carry on vital body functions.

18

EPILOGUE

YOUR
DOCTOR
AND YOU

Every chronic emphysema patient should have a doctor. Choosing a good doctor is a hit-and-miss proposition, just as finding a good auto mechanic or piano tuner is. All doctors are "good" for some of their patients and I am sure that some doctors are good for all of their patients.

In my fight with emphysema I have traveled about the country a great deal and, in so doing, I have had several doctors and quite a few specialists and consultants try their skills on my broken-down lungs.

There is one thing I want to set straight at the start; there is no doctor who can restore damaged lungs. Those poor misinformed individuals who change doctors every 30 days because they are not getting "better," should read this! After you have chosen your doctor, give him a chance. Emphysema is a very complex condition and each individual will vary somewhat because of all of the functions of the body that are involved. It may take a year for your doctor to reach a reasonable understanding of your particular problems. Your doctor should see you at regular intervals (at least once a month), even if you seem to be progressing satisfactorily.

You will want to work with your doctor at all times, telling him both the good and the bad. Above all, don't expect miracles. Emphysema is a condition which requires the patient to become essentially a doctor himself because it is a 24 hour a day type of problem.

We have written a small chapter in this book regarding the attitude of the patient. Now, however, I believe that it is not out of order to include a few items regarding your doctor's attitude and your attitude towards your doctor.

1. *Your doctor should give you confidence. If you have the slightest doubt regarding his advice or his ability, get another doctor in which you can have confidence.*

2. *Your doctor should have and show a keen interest in a long-range program for you. If he does not recognize that your emphysema is going to require a lengthy program of therapy, then he is not your doctor.*

3. *Beware of the "quick cure" specialist who knows all the answers and gives you the professional brush-off.*

4. *Once you have selected your doctor, believe him and do what he says—give it a try. Do not try to second guess him. Follow out all of his orders that you possibly can.*

5. *Always keep in mind that your doctor is only human. It is not in his power to perform miracles, so do not expect them.*

6. *Remember your doctor's instructions. He will not go over every phase of your trouble each time he sees you. For example: If your doctor*

spends 30 minutes with you planning a vitamin program, you are not to discontinue
postural drainage just because he has not mentioned it. Let each new set of instructions add
to your "get better" program, not replace last
week's instructions.

INDEX

INDEX